Only Joy Bites

Only Joy Bites

SHELLEY HILL

Healing House
PUBLISHING

First Published in Australia in 2025
by Healing House Publishing
www.healinghousepublishing.com

© Shelley Hill

All rights reserved. No part of this publication may be reproduced, stored in a retrieval system, or transmitted, in any form or by any means, electronic, mechanical, photocopying, recording, or otherwise, without the prior written permission of the publisher.

The National Library of Australia Cataloguing-in-Publication entry:

Title: Only Joy Bites
Author: Shelley Hill
Paperback ISBN: 978-1-7641185-8-3

Editor: Vanessa Barrington
Cover and Internal Design: Heidi Glasson

Healing House Publishing is committed to publishing works of quality and integrity. In that spirit, we are proud to offer this book to our readers; however, the story, the experiences, and the words are the author's alone.

*In loving memory
of my mother, Joy and father, Ken.*

PART ONE

The Armour of Love

1

Don't let yourself go

Dad carried the war on his skin - a tattoo of a red cross, a yellow shield haloed in blue, and *1967 Vietnam* inked across his forearm. As a kid, I placed him on a pedestal. It represented his time spent in battle as a young man. He was cool and not like any of my friends' fathers. He kept a pair of knuckle dusters in the glove box, just in case someone parked him in at the local RSL club and he could knock out their headlights. The car was decorated with trinkets: skull and crossbones, little metal badges superglued to the dash, and weird torches hanging out of the cigarette hole that you dared not touch.

It was about 11am and Dad was in his usual pair of stubbies, with a tanned, muscular physique and a beer in hand - a Foster's or VB. He looked a bit like Tom Selleck with his thick combed moustache and blow-dried wavy hair. I was ten years old and enjoying a day with Dad, which doesn't happen very often. Mum had left for work in her glamorous attire, carrying pages of squiggly shorthand notes for 'A Country Practice,' the TV series she worked for. That show lasted over a decade with 1088 episodes, depicting life in the fictional town of Wandin Valley. Mum often took home scripts to edit, and although she did most of the editing while working there, she stayed in her role of secretary due to a lack of confidence.

"I will give you a badge if you sing me a song," Dad said.

"Ok, Dad!" My voice pitched with anticipation.

"What song do I need to sing?" I asked.

"Who's the best dad in the world, that's old dadda wadda," he chanted.

This was a game he played with me when I was younger, so I thought it best to appease him today. He cracked his second beer, and I sang the words repeatedly, waiting patiently for the reward. I sang until I broke down into tears.

"You promised me the badge!"

"Mate, you don't get something for nothing in this world," he said. I looked down at my new badge; it was black, red, and white, with a ball and chain, and the words "The Rock of Alcatraz" embroidered on it. The tears stopped.

"Come on, let's take a drive to Centennial Park," Dad

said with a smirk.

He grabbed a roadie and chugged it down before we hit the Sydney Harbour Bridge. We arrived at the park, it was a cloudy day with drizzles of rain, so there weren't many people out feeding the ducks.

"Quick, I'll show you where the tortoises are," his voice a little rushed as he maneuvered his hand for me to follow him away from where we parked. We walked through a number of shrubs, and he led us to the muddy edge of a pond where mosquitoes circled us. I could feel their legs tickling the back of my neck as I instinctively slapped myself. They continued to land with readiness and leave disappointed; no blood drawn, nothing to nourish this tiny predator. Dad had a beer carton in his hand, but he was not carrying it like it were heavy. I assumed we would sit by the pond whilst he cracked another beer. I looked into the murky water to see a tiny reptilian head.

"Look, Dad. What's that?" I asked.

"Good spotting, just keep a lookout."

There was no one around. Dad waded into the pond in his denim blue stubbies. I watched as he reached in quickly with both hands and pulled out a tortoise, all four feet kicking, but Dad held on tight and popped it in the empty VB box.

"Are you allowed to do that, Dad?" I asked.

"You like tortoises, don't you?"

"Yes, but what are we going to do with him? Mum's gonna freak out."

"Don't worry, let's go back to the car," he said. I looked around, double-checking no one had seen us. We walked quickly back to the car.

"Matey, sit in the back and keep making sure he is ok and doesn't get out."

I jumped in the back seat next to the VB carton and opened the flap to peek. It was just a shell; his legs and head tucked safely inside himself.

"What are we going to call him?" I asked.

"What would you like to call him?" Dad replied.

"Mmm…Toby, I want to call him Toby," I decided. The three of us went back to our suburban backyard, where Dad had installed a pond amongst the fern trees. I was so excited to have my first pet. Dad went inside to get a beer, while I got comfortable handling Toby.

He was big, like the size of a dinner plate, and super strong. When I picked him up, his head popped out, along with his back legs, which fought furiously against my grip. He kicked and scratched at first, so I let him wander around surveying his new home.

I don't know how Mum's going to react when she gets home. I'm sure Dad will be in trouble, but I don't care. I'm just glad to have a little friend.

A few days later, Scunge arrived. He was a little worse for wear, with a mossy cover on his shell, so I grabbed a scrubbing brush and cleaned it off. I was not sure he liked this, as he seemed a little timid and kept inside his armour. Scunge and Toby quickly became my new friends and constant companions, wandering around the pond and hiding amidst the fern trees as I excitedly shared my secrets with them.

Each day brought a new adventure as I learned the quirks of my shelled friends—the way Toby would stretch his neck out, scanning for food, while Scunge preferred the quiet corners, his shell blending with the surroundings.

Dad never stopped tinkering with the backyard, adding little stepping stones, and drinking beer as I sat and watched my tiny world unfold. Mum, on the other hand, seemed less thrilled, often rolling her eyes at the mess the pond inevitably created. Yet, through all the chaos, those two tortoises taught me patience, wonder, and the joy of nurturing life.

As I grew older, my afternoons in the backyard shifted to evenings spent inside, where the realities of school and growing up slowly encroached. The tortoises remained, though, a quiet reminder of simpler times—a childhood filled with sadness and moments of unfiltered joy.

2

A Beautiful Facade

Mum walked quickly across the slate floor in her Tony Bianco wedged shoes, grey pencil skirt, and cashmere off-the-shoulder sweater. Her hair was big with dramatic, hooped earrings.

"I'm off to work, and I have left the latest edition of the calorie counter in your room. I think it might help knowing how many calories are in those Tim Tams you love, or the lollies you get after school," she said. "Just so you can keep an eye on it."

Everything was perfect, the painted nails, the polished silver necklace, the wedged shoes, and the Princess Diana hairstyle, slight wave, streaks and flicks above the shoulder. She would never leave the house without her 'face on'. I admired my mother's elegance, her beauty, and most of all her kindness. Kindness for mum was not just about being nice; it was caring and putting others first. Mum was a contestant in Miss Australia until her father died when she was twenty-one years old; she left the competition, and with her mother close by, they nursed him 'til his death.

"Thanks, Mum," I said and slowly walked upstairs to my tidy room. I could smell the ocean. I looked at my desk to find Allan Borushek's pocket calorie counter, last year's birthday present. It was a tiny book, and the latest edition came adorned with pictures of diet yoghurt, Lean Cuisine, equal sugar packets, and the evil KFC box. I quickly opened the book and flicked to Tim Tams.

One biscuit was 5.1 grams of fat, 12.1 grams of carbs, 0.3 grams of fibre and 98 calories!

***

I decided not to catch the bus today. Instead, I walked the steep stairs from Balmoral Beach that led me to Mosman High School. I had arrived at school anxious. At 10am, I piled into the bus that would take us to Balmoral Beach. The other kids were laughing and making jokes among themselves. I sat in silence, crammed against the window, wishing the bus would break down.

Now standing on the edge of an ocean pool at Balmoral

Beach in my multi-coloured tight Speedos, I was ready to dive into the dark green water. I couldn't see the bottom. The air was crisp as I started to switch off, my mind wandered to my mum's words.

"Do I look fat in this, Mum?"

"You feel fat because you are looking down at yourself."

These were Mum's words, said with pure honesty as she looked me up and down with 'that look'; eyebrows raised, head to one side and a deep sigh.

I was due to complete my Bronze Medallion, a requirement to participate in surf lifesaving patrol. This involved swimming 400 metres in nineteen minutes. I could barely make 25 metres without gasping for air!

A booming voice snapped me back to the moment.

"Ok, Shelley, you are next, and I want you to start with a safety jump."

I could feel everyone staring at me. My 17-year-old tummy felt bloated, my hands shook, and I just wanted to run.

I am much better at running. That's where I excel, not here.

I didn't like my swim instructor; her lips were thin and always pulled tight, and her physique was stocky with shoulders back. She had a strong and abrupt voice.

"I don't think you can do this," she said.

I felt something shift inside me. A safety jump is used if the depth of the water is unknown. I placed my right leg out towards the water, with my arms stretched out by my side. I was in and fueled with grunt as I swam to the nearest buoy and did exactly as instructed. Breathless and climbing out of the pool, I smiled to myself. I looked at my swimming instructor. Her face had softened. She pressed her thin lips together, corners slightly up, as she bowed her head.

'Fake it till you make it,' as Mum would say.

I headed to the change room with the other girls and hid in the corner, trying to peel my ugly swimsuit off.

There it is again, that belly. I wished it were toned and muscular, then I wouldn't have to ask Mum if I looked fat.

After I got changed, I scurried back to the bus to return to school. Later that afternoon, I took my time walking home, admiring seagulls, how white their feathers were, and the orange colour of their rubbery webbed feet. We lived a short walk from Balmoral Beach, so this distracted me for a short time. The sense of achievement soon disappeared as I got closer to home.

The Jacaranda trees lined both sides of the suburban street. The purple leaves either gently swayed in the breeze or were smashed up against the road by local traffic. Either way, I loved them. They made me feel nurtured and held. Mum was home early and drawing squiggles on a pile of papers when I walked in.

"Hi Mum, I checked out Tim Tam's in the book you gave me; I was horrified!" I said.

"It is good to know what you are eating, to keep track, to make sure you eat the right amount and exercise accordingly, so you don't put on weight. My mother always said stay slender, and don't let yourself go," Mum replied matter-of-factly.

I ran upstairs, got changed into my running gear, and grabbed my Walkman, which was a small cassette player with long headphones.

"I'm just off for a run, Mum, I won't be long," I called out.

Five hundred metres later, and I was at the beach.

Shoes off, soft sand is much harder and better for burning more calories.

I plugged the headphones into my Walkman. 'Eye of the Tiger' by Survivor came on, the theme song from the movie 'Rocky'. My feet glided through the sand with precision and ease. My heart pumped, and my mind went into an almost meditative state. I felt relaxed and present in the moment. After 30 minutes, I headed back home, exhilarated.

As I approached the dark green letterboxes, I saw Dad's car parked across the road. I felt my stomach sink, like I'd just swallowed a brick.

"Hey Matey," Dad stumbled out of the canary yellow Holden Gemini. I quickly scanned the entrance to our block of townhouses to see if any neighbours were around.

"How did you go today?" he slurred.

"Yeah, good Dad," I replied. I could tell he'd been at the RSL again, his second home. I ran around the back to quickly let Mum know Dad was drunk again.

Mum was in the kitchen cooking beef stroganoff, Dad's favourite meal. She looked outside the spacious window, the trees resisting the formidable force of the wind as it whipped unwelcoming through tender young branches, leaving discarded leaves torn apart in a sudden, violent onslaught.

Bang! Bang! Bang!

"Let me in!"

Dad pounded on the front door. He'd lost his keys. Mum opened it.

"Take your shoes off, you will dirty the floors! I've just cleaned them," she yelled. Dad stumbled in and went straight to the fridge. He grabbed a beer, choking its neck, and slumped into the brand-new Parker lounge with the beige floral pattern. Mum had saved up to buy it. It was a bit elite; being in Mosman, Mum needed to keep in with the status quo. My heart started pounding. Nights like this never ended well.

I went to my room to wait. A stillness descended, so quiet and peaceful until the next noisy interlude savagely embraced the innocent foliage outside again.

"Hey Matey, come and have a beer with your old man."

I reluctantly came out of my room and sat next to him on the couch. His moustache was covered in froth from his recent glug. His breath was stale as he leaned in to give me advice.

"Hey Matey, if you don't like a drink, you will never get into the police, and you will just be a dreamer, not a doer," he offered.

I longed for him to validate me, to see me as more than the boy he always wanted. Since Dad wanted a boy, he didn't quite know how to manage a girl, so he would take me to the local pubs around the Rocks area in Sydney, just like his old man did with him, and I would sit and watch him drink beer after beer. Dad's father also fought in World War II, and Pa was proud that Dad could drink at the age of 13.

I looked at the time. Dinner was always at 6pm, and it was 5.30pm.

I haven't set the table, that's my job.

I pulled out the beige placemats, a set of linen napkins and the sterling silver cutlery and set the table for three. Dad managed to get to the table. Dinner was served, and it was perfection as always; that was the only way Mum did things. Dad didn't say much; he was too drunk. I watched as his head got closer and closer to his plate, and just like that – SLOP! His forehead met the stroganoff.

Mum didn't eat much that night, and as I took the plates away, I saw her hiding in the laundry, secretly devouring a little biscuit.

"What's that you are eating, Mum?"

"Oh, it's just a bit of a meal replacement when I don't feel like a big meal," she replied. Limmits Biscuits were weight loss biscuits. I'd seen them advertised on TV. They promised to be chock-full of nourishment and assured the woman of the 80s they could 'eat and be slim'.

Gentle, soft rain fell outside, soaking into the grateful garden. The moistened leaves glisten with much-needed refreshment, as life itself was renewed.

No arguments tonight, I sighed in relief. Dad made his way upstairs to sleep it off. It was now just Mum and me, like always. Mum's eyes looked sad, and her shoulders hunched.

"Living with an alcoholic is like the man you knew has gone away, and you are left with a shadow, a substitute person, who you don't really know, or don't even like, for that matter. If it weren't for you, Shelley, I wouldn't be here," she said softly.

I felt like someone had just flipped me on my back, with a heavy boot and pushed hard into my throat. I couldn't speak.

3

Counting Calories

November 11, a few months later, Mum came home from work. It was my birthday, and she headed straight to the kitchen to cook. Dad and I were outside near the clothesline, crushing beer cans using our beer crusher—a metal plate bolted to the brick wall, cupped at the bottom with a lever that was the perfect size to fit a VB can. Dad placed his empty can under the lever and let me pull it down hard, crushing the can to a quarter of its size.

"I reckon we have about five bucks worth here, Matey," Dad said. We piled all the cans into a plastic bin, ready to take them to the recycle centre to get our five cents per tinny.

"Shelley, set the table, please," Mum's tone was clipped.

I rushed inside, grabbed the beige place mats, matched with the beige napkins, and the silver, polished cutlery. The napkins were ironed into a perfect rectangle. The Royal

Doulton white China plates with little silver flowers around the edge complemented my table decoration.

"Ken, can you do something? Clean the backyard, just do something apart from drink!" Mum screamed loud enough for the neighbours to hear. Dad grabbed another beer from the outdoor Esky, and I attended to Toby and Scunge.

"Mum, can Toby and Scunge come inside?"

"Yes, but they can only walk on the slate floor, not the carpet," she said. I brought the tortoises inside, letting them walk on the tiles. Mum cooked while Dad drank more beer and half-heartedly swept the back garden. I let the tortoises wander and placed them back in their pond.

At 6pm, dinner was served.

"Happy birthday, Matey," Dad said, handing me a Donkey Kong, an electronic handheld game. It was the first in the Game and Watch series with a double screen. It wasn't wrapped or in a box; he just handed it to me. I was bursting with excitement.

"Wow! Thanks, Dad, where did you get it?"

"It fell off the back of a truck," he said.

There must have been a lot of trucks losing their loads, cause Mum got these types of presents too; Oroton handbags and wallets, all with no packaging.

I wasn't complaining. Instead, I was excused from the table to wash up.

***

The next day, I walked to the bus stop and jumped on the bus. I walked into class, my favourite subject, English, yet my least favourite teacher, Mr Read. He was a big, burly, solid man with a thick brown and ginger beard. Mr Read loved to make students stand up and announce their answers to his questions. I looked out the window, hoping he wouldn't choose me.

"Shelley, stand up. What do you think the answer is to my question?" I nervously stood upright. The other students' necks arched back, staring at me, ready for the most pertinent answer.

"What was the question again, Mr Read?" I froze as I felt the heat rise behind my ears, burning as it crept into my neck. My cheeks and face were on fire. Before I could open my mouth again, the classroom filled with the laughter of teenagers responding appropriately to Mr Read's ego.

"I don't know the answer, Sir," I replied.

I sat back down, looking out the window to the barren concrete playground and started reciting silently in my head.

I ate half a piece of toast for breakfast, then I had a handful of blueberries at morning break, half a Tim Tam, half an egg and lettuce sandwich with one Jatz cracker for lunch.

Then five minutes later:

I ate half a piece of toast for breakfast, then I had a handful of blueberries, half a Tim Tam, half an egg and lettuce sandwich with one Jatz cracker for lunch.

This happened every day until I fell asleep. If I ate something 'bad', I would make a deal with myself to train harder, faster or longer as punishment.

3.30pm and I was at the bus stop. The 257 bus from Chatswood to Balmoral arrived. I started to sweat, clammy, and my vision blurred. I could see the other kids stepping onto the bus. Everything went dark. I woke up on the bitumen. There was no bus, no students. I gathered my school bag and walked down the steep hill home.

I began to faint a lot at the Royal Easter Show and anywhere with crowds. Mum took me to her doctor to figure out why I was fainting; the result, hypoglycemia. (My prediction was a little different: a psychosomatic response to internalising trauma, and a way to shut it down). The fainting stopped as soon as I was old enough to leave home.

I walked inside feeling embarrassed. There was no one home.

Why didn't anyone ask if I was okay at the bus stop? Was this another lesson that Mum had taught me? Do not embarrass yourself in public, and fake it 'til you make it, while staying slender?

I ran to my room, got into my training gear, ran back downstairs and grabbed the skipping rope from my allocated space in the outdoor shed. I had to do one thousand skips before Mum and Dad got home from work, and if I tripped, I had to do ten extra punishment skips.

4

The Dodgy Lock

A few months later, Dad started taking the garbage out and not coming home. Mum never said much about it, yet this day was different. Mum was upset - really upset. It was 7.30am and I looked outside my bedroom window to see the yellow Gemini coming down the drive, the brakes screeching as it got closer to the undercover park. I could hear Mum's feet pacing in her bedroom next to mine. I placed my ear to the wall, with my left hand over my left ear, to hear more sound effects.

Is she crying?

No. She was sobbing. The sobbing that lifts your chest up and down so hard that all the air in your nostrils gets pushed out, silently, and then a long sigh at the end. I imagined tears running down her face.

What has happened? Was this an example of another lesson? Don't show negative emotions, like fear, vulnerability; show a face of strength and courage. Mum didn't want me to hear her crying. I thought Dad was coming home from night shift at the fire station?

I could hear the keys jiggling in the front door. My bedroom door was closed. Mum walked past, heading downstairs, her footsteps soft. I slowly opened my bedroom door and crept across the hall to my safe space, the bathroom with the dodgy door handle. I pushed the long handle in and twisted it up so that it locked. I waited.

"Where the fuck have you been, Ken?"

Uh oh. Mum rarely swore. He has been on night shift, Mum, leave him alone!

I slowly opened the door so I could peer over the timber slatted staircase. Dad was in his fire brigade uniform.

"What do you mean? I've been at work! What the fuck are you on about? For fuck's sake!"

Mum wasn't sobbing anymore; she was about to lose it.

"Really, Ken, really? You didn't actually go to work, so where were you? Where were you, Ken?"

"Fucking leave me alone, you crazy bitch, I need to sleep," he screamed.

Voices raised, raging anger filled the house.

"You stink of booze, where were you?"

I could see Dad taking a few steps to get upstairs. I ran

back to my bathroom and turned the handle. I was safe.

"You fucking liar! I called the station, and this time your mates told me the truth, you were not rostered!" Mum screeched at the top of her voice.

I heard a thud.

Shit, I'd better help.

I gingerly opened the bathroom door. Dad had his hand on Mum's throat, and Mum was punching him in the arm.

"Stop, stop, please!" I yelled.

They both stopped, and Dad brushed past me. The whiff of beer wafted over me. Mum was slumped, sobbing on the corner step.

"Sorry, Shelley."

"That's okay, Mum," I replied.

"You can't stay here. Grab your things, and I'll take you to Sue and Brooke's house."

"Ok. Mum, will you be ok?"

"I'll be fine," she replied. I packed a small overnight bag and met Mum downstairs. We both walked out in silence, and once in the car, it was a short five-minute drive up to Sue and Brooke's house. Sue was Mum's best friend, and we had all known each other since I was two years old. As a result, their family unit, including John, Sue's husband, and Robbie, Brookes' brother, was familiar and nurturing. I waved Mum goodbye.

Not wanting to make conversation, I went for a walk in the paved garden instead. I placed my shaking hands out in front of me. I did not know how to soothe the turbulence pulsing through my body. I stood still, looking up at the trees surrounding me, their gentle sway and rustle dropping my heart rate ever so slightly. I sat on the ground and took a few deep breaths. I sensed something bigger than me, a belonging, a knowing. It felt soothing.

***

I had been at Sue's place for a few days before Mum decided it was time for me to come home. Dad was living with his mother in the eastern suburbs of Sydney. I missed crushing cans; I missed the family dinners. I would often go and play with Toby and Scunge, feeding them and watching them walk around the backyard. Mum had started drinking heavily; it was her way of coping with Dad's new affair.

Mum and I started ordering the evil KFC meals. Mum would have a few mouthfuls of coleslaw and bean salad, a few glasses of wine, and I was allowed a couple of chicken wings whilst we listened to the Carpenters. It was our regular Friday night together. As the days passed, Mum cried a lot, and Gran, her mother, would often come over. Dad came and went, dropping in to see me and check on

Mum. At times, he would sleep over, and then one day, he never came back.

"Mum, Mum!" I yelled, but she didn't respond. No movement was seen; her body was laid to one side, still and lifeless on the carpeted floor. Her face looked pale. I touched her arm with my trembling hand; it felt clammy and cold. I looked around the bedroom she no longer shared with Dad. The bed was made, with the sheets tight around the corners, the doona and pillowcases were ironed and matching.

Nothing out of the ordinary here.

I glanced to my left, and I saw a wine glass, half-filled with a bold golden Chardonnay.

Still nothing out of the ordinary here.

"Mum, wake up, please," my voice quivered. Her body was limp as she mumbled something I couldn't make sense of. Out of the corner of my eye, I saw a box of Valium, the foil blisters popped open, and the empty bottle of McGuigan's Chardonnay. I froze.

Who do I call?

I called Dr Graham, her local GP. She saw him every week, they were close, and within minutes, I heard the wail of a siren, the pounding of feet heading towards our front door… her body being carried out on a stretcher. I stood quietly alone, my body shaking as tears fell unashamedly down my already wet cheeks. Deep sadness etched in the corner of my mouth; my eyes filled with pain and fear. A phone call to Gran resulted in Sue coming to collect me, and that's where I stayed.

* * *

A few days later, I went to visit Mum with Gran at a psychiatric facility. It was an unusual place; the entrance was encapsulated by a pond with turtles in it. The turtles' hard shells protected their soft, vulnerable body. I was familiar with these creatures, so I moved closer to the pond and saw a tiny head quickly retract into its protective armour. My fascination was softly interrupted by Gran's words.

"Isn't this a lovely place, dear? Look at those turtles," she said.

The word "lovely" was not something I associated with a Psychiatric Facility, but Gran was trying to make small talk.

Mum would recount stories of other inpatients, rushing to get the lowest calorie snack in a desperate attempt to maintain some sort of control and skeletal frame. About a week later, Gran and I had a formal meeting with the psychiatric doctor.

"Hello, Mrs Walsh, you must be Joy's mother? And Shelley? Joy's daughter?" he asked.

"Yes," we said at the same time.

"Joy is doing ok, she is quite thin, but she is trying to eat. Joy tells us that her husband, Ken, has left her. Joy also told us that she has been restricting her food and using alcohol to cope. We have diagnosed Joy with anxiety, depression and anorexia nervosa. With some medication and psychiatric treatment outside of here, she will be able to go home."

"Thank you, doctor. Joy has been quite the handful, especially as a teenage girl. She had a good upbringing, yet she always compared herself to her brother. She lacked so much confidence, and one day she threw herself in front of a bus on Military Road," Gran says.

"Well, with the right kind of treatment, we should be able to help Joy," the doctor replied.

The news was difficult to digest. I was unaware of my mother's battle with anorexia over the previous years. I just thought she was in fashion, elegant and slender. Now looking back, Mum was losing weight, and I was becoming more anxious, spending a lot of time away from home. I had begun to feel myself withdrawing, feeling alone, but I was too ashamed to tell anyone what was happening. Calorie counters and scales soon became my friend as I obsessed over my body. I counted the calories in everything I ate into a religious, compulsive pattern of order and control. I created a personal food pyramid of tiny snacks and continued to recite it over and over in my mind as I dissociated from the external world.

I began to spend a lot of time at Nan's house. She lived next door to Rhonda, Dad's sister. Rhonda's two daughters, Kim and Julie and I were close. I was the eldest. I never wanted to go back home. I wanted Rhonda to be my Mum; she was nurturing and affectionate. I always compared her to Mum. Mum and Dad rarely showed affection; it was just how it was.

* * *

That year at Christmas, Mum and Dad got back together. I was excited to spend it at Nan's. Her house was huge, with the lounge room walls thickly stained from tobacco, and she always overcooked the broccoli until it was yellow, but I didn't care; I felt at home. I even had my own room. Dad, Mum and I walked down the hallway towards the Christmas table. I saw a large bowl of lollies centred on top of the plastic floral tablecloth, surrounded by plastic bowls of salads. Mum was talking to Rhonda.

"Hey Nan, can we have a lolly?" I asked on behalf of myself, Kim and Julie.

"Of course you can," she replied. The three of us grabbed

a handful of red frogs, teeth, strawberries and cream, gummy bears and chocolate freckles. I caught Mum's face from the corner of my eye. Her jaw was tight, and her face looked fierce.

"Shelley, come here, please," she said. I immediately walked towards her, and as I stopped, she pointed down the hallway.

"You know better than to eat lollies before lunch, now go to your room. You won't be having lunch with us today," she said.

Ashamed, I walked to my room located at the end of the hall, near the front door. A large mirror was placed over a shiny veneer dresser with ornate gold handles. The wardrobe on either side had Pa's clothes in it. He had fought in World War II before joining the Navy. He was a big drinker and died a few years ago. I lifted my t-shirt, standing side on in front of the mirror and pushed out my belly.

Mum's right. I'll never lose weight if I continue to do things like this.

After lunch, Rhonda came to see me.

"Are you okay, sweetie?" she asked.

"Yes, I'm fine," I said.

"Come and join us."

I walked back down to the dining room. Julie was clearing the plates as I approached. I spotted my bowl covered in cling wrap, some ham, chicken, potato and salad, with one ring of white bread. I felt anxious and embarrassed to eat alone.

"I'm pretty full after the lollies. I might have it later, Nan, if that's ok?"

"Are you sure?" she asked kindly.

"Yeah, I am sure," I said, as I noticed Dad twisting another top off his beer.

5

The Cops

My parents officially divorced when I turned 18. Dad left Mum for the Irish woman, Alice whom he'd been having an affair. The family house was sold, and Dad returned to the eastern suburbs to buy a home there. My mum bought a unit in Mosman, where we lived together. A year later, with a burning desire to embark on a career, I was accepted into the NSW Police Force. I endured a rigorous and physically demanding entry test at the training grounds in Redfern, Sydney. As part of my eligibility, I had to scale a six-foot wall. I spent hours practising, running towards the wall at full speed, trying to grab the top and lift my body weight over it. I practised 'til my wrists and hands were bruised and bleeding.

***

At 19, I found myself in Goulburn, a regional city in the southern tablelands of New South Wales, about two hours from home. The strong, turbulent wind rapidly changed the manicured landscape. It was bitterly cold, and I was frozen with fear the morning I walked into an auditorium full of young men and women all with the same purpose: to become a NSW police officer. Dad's words rang loudly in my head.

You will never get into the police. It's a boy's club.

Dad was a fireman, and he understood the male culture. But in 1990, things were changing, and women were more accepted. We were assigned a group based on the first letter of our surname, and once we split into groups, I made friends with a woman who was two years older than me, Debbie. She was born in New Zealand, and we instantly clicked. At our first dinner, we sat next to each other. It was a self-serve buffet style, and I was just happy to be away from my parents. The dining room was cold and sterile. I felt like I was on one of those TV shows where prisoners share a meal amongst a sea of different personalities and stories.

"Hey Shell, is it ok if I call you Shell?" Debbie asked.

"Yes, of course," I replied.

"So, what made you join the cops?" she asked.

"Well… I always wanted to help people. You know, when I think of the police, I think they are there to help, right? And to be honest, I couldn't wait to leave the chaos of home life behind," I paused nervously before continuing. "My dad said I would never make it, but here I am!"

I giggled nervously.

"So, how about you, Debbie, why the cops?"

"I've just seen a lot of shit go down in New Zealand, and I came here for an escape, and I guess I just wanted to make a difference, hey, plus my fiancé is a cop."

It was a long day, and Debbie and I headed to our rooms, just down the hall from each other. I opened the door to my room, which had a single bed to the right and a desk near the window to the left, with a carpeted floor and an old-style country theme. The room had a view of the frosty trees and a shared bathroom. My first night felt strange. I unpacked my bag, put my pyjamas on and jumped into bed. I wasn't sure about being a cop after looking around at all the tough-looking guys and girls throughout my orientation. I placed my hand on my heart to feel the thumping inside my chest. I closed my eyes with pure exhaustion and fear of what tomorrow might bring.

Two days later, it was time for the room inspection. This happened every so often and usually by surprise.

"Knock knock, room inspection."

Sergeant Trevors walked in with a serious job to do. He was burly, fat gutted with a blank face. I stood tall, shoulders back.

"Morning, Sir," I said.

He grunted as his eyes scanned the single bed dorm, bed tightly made, desk tidy, pens away, books stacked in order of size.

"Mmm, make sure your shoes look better than that before you come to breakfast," he barked. I felt intimidated and scared, yet I knew this dominance was part of the process to shape me into a tough cop. I had the same grumbling in my gut, just like being back at home.

"Yes, Sir," I replied quickly, grabbing my polishing stocking with trembling hands. I spat on the tip of the black school-like leather shoe and started rubbing vigorously. The idea was to create a half-moon, shiny tip using an old stocking, saliva, and considerable effort. Above my desk were extracts of Criminal Law, along with the very important phrase that must be learnt verbatim, 'You are under arrest, you have the right to remain silent, but whatever you do and say, may be used as evidence, do you understand that?'

After breakfast, I met the other classmates on the parade ground. We lined up tallest to shortest, men and a handful of women.

"Okay, class 247. A-TEN-SION!" Sergeant Trevor drew the word out loudly, snapping it short at the end.

We brought our right foot in to meet the left, with the left arm stiff by our side, and our right hand swiftly met the forehead.

"Do not move unless I tell you to do so!" he barked. The slightest wiggle could result in punishment push-ups and humiliation for the offender. Nervous energy ran through me like a faulty electrical cable, pulsating and zapping at my heart centre. The only way to handle my inner turmoil was what I knew best: survive by remaining in total control. I was calm and determined on the outside, ever prepared to be undeterred by any change in circumstances. My body was rigid, my shoulders back, as the sun beat down; I could barely breathe. I was on the verge of fainting by the time Sgt. Trevors dismissed us. I squatted down and pretended to tie my shoelace.

As the months passed, I began to feel like I had a sense of family. I bonded with some other students and would often sneak out at night, crossing the paddock of cows, to arrive at Flamingoes, the local nightclub. Most of the students from the force were there. We would all let loose, dance and drink until we got kicked out at 11pm, and stumble our way back to our rooms, or someone else's room.

After a particularly big night, I woke up with a hangover and headed to the dining room for breakfast with Debbie. Within minutes, Sgt. Trevors walked in with his booming voice.

"Everyone, get into your training gear after breakfast and meet at the assembly area. 8am sharp," he said with a smile.

We assembled in our training gear and all lined up as instructed, most of us looking a little worse for wear.

"Right, follow me! We are going for a 10-kilometre run," shouted Sgt. Trevors. Within a few kilometres, a few students peeled off to the side of the road to vomit. The real cops who mentored us knew exactly where we had been last night.

Near the end of my stay at Goulburn, I had to learn how to fire a Smith and Wesson revolver. We would do simulation exercises where we would enter a staged building where violent offenders were hiding. Cardboard cutouts of priests would pop up, or men with angry faces pointing a gun, as we hid behind corners and approached each scenario with caution and readiness, making sure not to shoot the priest. This insular environment was fun, and there were no real "baddies" to confront. I studied hard, passed all my assessments and drank a lot of beer without vomiting on the early morning runs. The uniform in the 90s was considerably old-fashioned. A pair of culottes, which was a mix of a pant leg and a skirt over the top. A pair of stockings and dress shoes, ready to chase bad guys over a fence. The baton was tucked closely by my side and reached down as far as my knee. The hat was similar to that of a bowling hat, a short brim and a big top, once again completely impractical to be walking the streets, chasing offenders, or just being comfortable for the majority of the shift.

Perhaps that is what drew me to the police force at the age of 19. They looked polite, dressed well, and took care of the neighbourhood. I wanted to believe that I was helping people, and that was my focus.

I graduated with a sense of achievement, and I was posted to a sleepy little station on Sydney's affluent North Shore in Mosman. It was an old house converted into a police station, located a few minutes' drive from Taronga Zoo. Break-and-enters were high on the job list, along with the odd emu escaping from the zoo. Mosman had its fair share of journalism juice, like the 'Granny Killer' John Wayne Glover, an English-Australian serial killer who was convicted of murdering six elderly women over fourteen months. I arrived at Mosman in 1990, just as the case was being wrapped up. The morning Victor Chang was murdered on July 4, 1991, at 8am, I had just finished the night shift. Victor Chang was a pioneer in cardiac surgery, and his amateur killers tried to extort money in broad daylight, with sixteen witnesses. Two shots to the head, and Dr Chang died tragically.

I hated night shift; I struggled to stay awake. My nickname was Noddy because I would fall asleep at any chance I could, whether in the passenger seat of a police car or curled up on the floor while on station duty. One evening, my female offsider, Senior Constable Webster, and I were driving around looking for signs of potential crims. It was about 3am, and I could feel my head nodding back and forth as the motion of the car put me into a deep sleep. I heard the screech of the siren, and the handbrake jerked into the upright position.

"Quick, get out," Webster yelled.

I fell flat onto the bitumen of a quiet suburban street. I wriggled my legs, noticing for the first time that my shoelaces were tied together. Webster was bent over with laughter. Somehow, she managed to tie my laces together, wacked the sirens on and pretended we had a job, as she screamed for me to get out of the police car. They were the fun times; police officers used to love playing practical jokes on each other. There was a bond between most cops; we had each other's backs, and when the shit hit the fan, we had to rely on our partner.

6

This is Not Me.

Four years later, the whole idea of helping people had long been overshadowed by an institution that was full of racism, homophobia and false superiority. I was still the shy kid, but now I was hiding behind a badge and a gun. My ego liked being a police officer, but my soul and spirit were grinding up against this idealism. I had empathy for the kids on the street who would get locked up. I wanted to understand them, not just treat them like scum. I hated to see other officers belt offenders with phone books and humiliate people with mental health issues. If I just shut up, had a beer or three after work, then the camaraderie enveloped me, and I felt safe and accepted. This meant everything, as I hadn't always felt safe as a child.

Around this time, a new graduate arrived, a young

country girl from regional NSW. Constable Toni Brown had moved from Coolah to the big smoke of Sydney. When Toni arrived at Mosman, I poked my head around the corner of the change room to clap my eyes on the newbie. I sensed a kindred spirit.

"Hi, my name is Shelley," I said as I walked out to introduce myself.

"Hi, I'm Toni," she said, placing her fingers over her mouth. Later, I learned that she was self-conscious about her bucked teeth. Toni looked like a beautiful mix of Eurasian and an Inuit. She had dark hair, small almond eyes and high cheekbones. We became inseparable and couldn't wait to be rostered on the same shift. To hide our attraction to each other, we would hide in the women's change room and kiss, until one day Senior Constable Rodd swung the door open.

"Busted," he chuckled as he walked away, leaving us terrified of the repercussions of rife homophobia, not only in the station but also in the broader police community. I ended up dating a few male cops, trying desperately to be straight, until it led to nasty messages in my pigeonhole calling me a 'Lesbian mole'. Toni and I were 'outed' and our attraction led to an everlasting friendship.

Back then, earning an extra stripe on my shoulder - marking five years as a Police Officer - meant extra study through Charles Sturt University. The requirements have since changed, but at the time, it meant I needed to complete a Diploma of Policing, including an assignment on a current issue within the Local Area Command. I decided to address the issues surrounding the gay 'beat' at Obelisk Beach in Mosman, and my Commander was to oversee the assignment. We would often get rostered to patrol the toilet blocks at night as part of our evening job list.

One warm summer's evening, I was paired up with one particular Senior Constable, a rather skinny guy for his six-foot-tall height. We had not worked together before. About 8pm, we jumped in the police truck and drove down to Obelisk Beach to catch the 'poofters'.

"I don't mind lesbians, but these fucking fags, they should just go back to Oxford Street and get out of our area," he said. I said nothing. It was a well-known fact that many of the men having sex in public toilets were often married with children and did not identify as gay, and that they would not get HIV or AIDS, as that only happened to the real gay men on Oxford Street. The risk of being assaulted, murdered or charged with offensive behaviour was very clear, and our job was to intimidate and harass them, which only reinforced the distance between the police and the queer community in the early 90s.

As we headed towards the toilet block, I noticed two

men hanging around. One guy was short and muscly with a tight pair of shorts, the other was skinnier and wore a pair of boardshorts and a loose singlet. I walked beside my colleague, waiting to see how we would approach the men.

"What are you guys doing here?" my colleague said.

"Nothing, Constable. Just having a chat," the muscly guy said.

"We don't want your kind around here, so best you fuck off back to Oxford Street, before you get bashed," my colleague said harshly.

The men scurried away. We had successfully done our job for the night and ticked that off the list. That was then, and while such a patrol was apparently not uncommon at the time, that's not the way police act now.

The next morning, Toni and I caught up over coffee.

"Oh my god, you won't believe the job I went to the other night. This guy had gassed himself in his car. He had been there for weeks and literally had fluorescent green goo running down his leg. When the contractors came to collect the body, he exploded!" Toni said in an excited tone. She loved the fascination of a decaying human body, and so did I. Toni could have her lunch break while a guy was hanging, waiting for the government contractors, but then again, she came from the country and was accustomed to tying string around sheep's balls until they dropped off.

"Wow," I said. "I handed in my assignment today, the one I did on the gay beat. The Commander didn't look too impressed," I said.

We shared a few stories over coffee and discussed heading out to a girls' night in Newtown. It was a Wednesday night at the Bank Hotel, a women-only event. We had a few drinks and forgot about exploding bodies and homophobic cops.

I lasted five years at Mosman before being transferred to another station. I suspect the Commander wasn't that unhappy to see me go, but I'll never know now.

7

The Willie Suit

Policing in the Inner West was very different to the white Caucasian affluence of Mosman. The cops were hardened, and the disparity between the police and the Indigenous population was like an open wound that refused to heal.

In my first week, I was rostered with Constable Peter Forsyth. He was a tall, kind man from Toowoomba in Queensland. I felt safe with Pete and grateful to be shown the ropes by such a gentle human. On our first shift together, we arrived at the paddy wagon, and I noticed a large suit in the back.

"Hey Pete, what's with the big suit in the back?" I asked. Pete smiled.

"That's the Willie suit, don't worry, you will get to meet

Willie, he is a regular customer. Get in and I'll explain."

Pete got in the driver's seat and we started to patrol the back streets of Glebe, where most of the houses or units were run down, with empty beer bottles and plastic chairs out the front. This was the housing commission area. As we drove up to the main road where the trendy cafes lined the streets, Pete started to tell me about Willie.

"Willie is well known to police, and if he gets aggravated in any way by members of the public or police, he puts his hands down his pants and pulls out his poos and throws it at us or anyone nearby. The suit in the back is to protect us from his shit, cause that little fucker will just poo on command, and you better duck and weave," he explained.

"That is gross! I hope we don't get a Willie job today, Pete!"

Pete laughed and ordered us a coffee. We worked well together. No one called us a copper cunt, or made snorting pig-like noises, and no one spat on us. It was a good day.

Very early into my time with the police, I heard some horror stories from colleagues. In one particular story, another cop told me about being rostered with a colleague who used to find it amusing to tease people of different nationalities, threatening to give them a ticket for not having their eyes fully open while driving.

I cringed hearing these stories. There were a few good

police officers that I liked to work with, who were kind and real, but inevitably, I began to hate my job. I loathed going to work, I was anxious most of the time, and I was drinking and partying to escape the tightness in my chest and the reality of my life. My inner mind ran like a rat on a mouse wheel most of the time I was on shift.

One night, we were called to the train station after someone jumped in front of the train. Approaching the scene, the darkness of the night was illuminated by flashing red and blue lights. Police cars, ambulance vehicles, and blue and white checkered tape surrounded the railway tracks. The smell of burning rubber was mixed with grease and oil from the train's sudden braking.

"Constable, grab a crime scene bag. We need some help getting this guy off the track. Actually, grab a few bags, he is in pieces," yelled a male voice from the Crime Scene Unit.

Without hesitation, I descended onto the track, gloves on and bent down to place bloody fingers, a hand, and squishy brain matter into bags. That was the end of my night shift, and at the end of it, deep exhaustion consumed me. I did everything to try and stay awake while driving home, nodding off at the wheel, the music blaring, the windows down, anything that would get me home.

ONLY JOY BITES

* * *

A few months later, I received a phone call from a female police officer who was a close friend of Pete's. I placed my hands on my forehead and cried. I couldn't believe it. February 27, 1998. Pete was out having drinks after work with Semps, Jason Semple, and Nifty; Brian Neville, two other police officers who worked with me. They were at a local pub, dressed in half-uniforms, wearing navy trousers and plain T-shirts. Pete invited the boys back to his house, where he lived with his wife and two children. They were within a hundred metres of his home when a young male named Murray Hearne asked the boys if they wanted to score drugs. The cops flashed their badges, and the night turned ugly and fatal.

Flashes of his gentle smile engulfed my mind.

"Pete, not Pete. Why Pete, why?' I cried. I cried for his family, and I also cried for my grief. The last eight years of policing fell from my eyes like shards of glass onto my lap as reality hit.

Peter Forsyth was stabbed twice in the heart, and Jason Semple was stabbed in the stomach. Brian Neville went in pursuit of Murray Hearne. Pete was 28 years old. Murray Hearne was eventually arrested when the story aired on "Australia's Most Wanted." I attended the state funeral for Pete at St Mary's Cathedral, and people came from all over for it. It was epic, the story had touched the hearts of many. People spilled outside the arched doorways to pay respect to Pete; a police officer, a son, a husband and a father. I sat in the church pew wearing my full uniform, shoes polished to perfection, and gazing at the large photo of Pete. His smile and lovable nature made me wonder: *Is this job worth risking my life?*

8

Mardi Gras

It was my second day of annual leave, and Mardi Gras was on. In the 90s, there was only one place to be: the dance parties on Oxford Street, Sydney. It was fun, queer and outrageous. Dressed in a pair of cut-off denim shorts and a black singlet, it was 6pm, and things were just kicking off. I was invited to someone's house for drinks. I didn't know them, but I accepted the invitation to watch the parade. The large, cream-coloured terrace with wrought-iron fencing overlooked Oxford Street, offering prime viewing for the Mardi Gras Parade. I brought a few beers with me and made awkward conversations with strangers. A mixed crowd of gay boys and lesbians. Shortly after I arrived, a hand tapped me on the shoulder.

"Hey, there are lines going in the kitchen if you want one?"

"Lines of what?" I asked.

"Oh, honey, it's just a cheeky line of speed," said the handsome man in tight glittery shorts.

"Sure, of course," I said. I grabbed my beer and took a few slow steps towards the stairs that led to the kitchen downstairs. The microwave was running.

"Whose turn is it to rack up?" a voice yelled out. As I reached the bottom of the stairs, I turned to see a woman with short blonde hair, green eyes, and a toned, tanned appearance. She was wearing leather shorts and a leather bra. My stomach fluttered as she handed me a rolled-up $20 note. The microwave stopped running, and a dinner plate with nothing on it came out. I watched closely as white powder was tipped out onto the heated plate. A driver's licence was used to make lines about 5 cm long.

"Off you go," said the attractive blonde girl who handed me the note. I placed a portion of the rolled-up note in my right nostril, bent down and started to trace the white powder as I inhaled. I did it a few times to get it all up; it stung, and my eyes began to water as I lifted my head from the plate.

"Thanks," I said.

My body tingled, and my head bounced to the music out on the street. I had never felt anything like the rush before. The shy, awkward kid faded into the background. I had my own uniform on now, not the one with the insignia

"Culpam Poena Premit Comes" (punishment swiftly follows crime), or the blue shirt and pants, with a Smith and Wesson revolver attached to my right hip, or the one that masked my insecurities and told me I was powerful. No, I was high, euphoric, and confident, and I was going to ask the hot blonde note roller her name.

"Hi, I'm Shelley."

"Hi Shelley, I'm Lynn."

She had an accent. We watched the parade together and had a few more lines before walking to the biggest dance party I had ever seen. Just before we walked in, Lynn opened the palm of her hand and showed me a white pill.

"Want one?" she asked.

"What is it?" I replied.

"It's an ecky, an ecstasy pill. Mm… maybe just have half if you are not used to them?"

I erred on the side of caution and took half as suggested.

As the pill kicked in, I grabbed Lynn and kissed her on the lips. We hugged and kissed for what seemed like hours. This was all so new and exciting and unlike me, the rigid and self-controlled type.

"I'll meet you guys at the left-hand side of the stage, third pylon in. Kylie is performing tonight, we can't miss it," yelled Lynn's friend.

The night turned into daylight, and we all left to freshen up for the day party. Outfit change, a few lines, shot of tequila, back to the dance floor. A tall, handsome gay man started dancing with me. He looked at me with curiosity as he wiggled himself around me with his hands in the air.

"Hey, you look familiar. You look like the cop who came to my work the other day and ordered a coffee?"

"No, that's not me. Must be my lookalike," I said with a grin.

We spent the next six hours dancing, talking, drinking, popping pills and snorting lines of speed in the toilet cubicle. Josh and I became remarkably close after that night, and would hang out together every chance we could, trying all the restaurants and the latest gay bars. One day, I turned up at his quaint little café in my police uniform.

"I knew it!" Josh ran his gayest run towards me and wrapped his arms around my shoulders. He whispered in my ear, "Shit, darl, what about all the drugs we took the other night?"

"That was weeks ago, and I was on leave. The drugs are out of my system now," I said.

9

Good Work Matey

After a few months back at work, I was done with getting spat at, snorted at, kicked, abused, picking body parts off train tracks from a suicide, attending horrific motor vehicle accidents and domestic violence scenes. I volunteered to work for a few months at the Exhibit Centre, where I received crime-related items from other police to store until court cases. This included weapons, jewellery, drugs, clothing, cash, etc. It wasn't thrilling, but it was simple, and I didn't have to patrol the streets. When my dad heard about the large collection of weapons at the centre, he got excited and even visited me at the counter one day.

It was 8am on a Sunday, and I was the only one at work. There wasn't much to do when there weren't crime scene articles to check in. The front door opened, and Dad walked in, looking a little dishevelled, with bloodshot eyes and shaking hands.

"What are you doing here, Dad?" I asked.

"Just thought I would come and check this place out," he said as I frowned in confusion.

"Hey Matey, do you reckon you could get me one of those guns from out the back?"

"Are you serious, Dad? These weapons are to be used in court. They have been used in a crime, like murder!" I said, shaking my head at his ridiculous question. He thought all cops were 'on the take' because he'd seen a lot of that working in the fire brigade. Dad walked away disappointed. He had a lot of guns at home, fifteen in fact, that ranged from rifles, pistols, magnums, and homemade numbers that used gunpowder. He acquired these during the war somehow. I felt bad that I couldn't get something for Dad, after all, he'd given me plenty of things 'off the back of a truck' over the years. I searched the storeroom and checked the "To Be Destroyed" book. Once the court cases were over, we usually took any weapons to the firearms department to be destroyed. I grabbed a silencer that Dad could attach to one of his rifles to muffle the sound of a gunshot. I quickly stepped outside and placed it in the boot of my car.

That evening, I went around to Dad's for a beer. His partner Alice was home, making dinner. I grabbed two stubbies of Carlton Draught, one for me and one for Dad, out of my bag. We sat outside around the pool.

"I got you a present, Dad," I said.

He beamed with a smile and replied, "Did you get your old man a gun?"

"No, Dad, but I got you this," I said, pulling out the silencer from my shopping bag.

"You little beauty! Good work, Matey." Dad seemed happy with me, as he held the piece in his hand and examined it closely. He slapped me on the back. I had always felt not good enough around my father. He would say things like, "You have it in here, placing his hand on his heart, but you haven't got it up here," as he tapped his temple.

I feel stupid. I'm not street smart.

Dad thought he was clever when he stole something from the fruit and veg store or a DVD from JB Hi-Fi, because in Dad's eyes, everyone was out to rip him off and given my father's height, tattoos and intimidating demeanour, no one fucked with Kenny.

"Get me another beer, and yourself one too and come into the garage," he said as he walked into the enclosed garage, where some of his guns were hanging on the wall. He had rifles, including single-barreled, double-barreled, and bolt-action guns, proudly on display. He polished them every other day. As I got to the fridge to grab beers, I asked Alice if she needed a hand.

"No, just go and be with your Dad," she said a little abruptly. In the meantime, Dad had attached the silencer to his bolt-action rifle and set up four empty cans of beer in a row.

"Let's have a game and see who can shoot the most beer cans."

"What about the neighbours? Are you sure this will work?" I said.

"That's what the silencer is for, Matey! I'm just using a little slug for the rifle, it's not a big deal, don't worry," Dad said.

I rubbed my fingers together in anticipation. Even though I fired my Smith and Wesson revolver at pistol training days in the police, Dad never allowed me to touch his guns for the simple fact that he didn't want them in the wrong hands, the hands of a novice. Dad's voice was loud and clear.

"Place the butt of the rifle into your shoulder, near your armpit. Push it in tight, now close your left eye and look down the barrel. Place your right index finger on the trigger, but don't pull it yet. Find the sights and see those two bits that stick up at the end of the barrel?" he continued.

"Yes," I said, determinedly with confidence.

"Ok, now aim for the middle of the beer can and keep steady. Once you are steady, pull the trigger," he instructed.

Ping! The little bullet skimmed the left-hand side of

the beer can. I quickly turned and looked at Dad.

"That's ok mate, I'll give you a demo," he said in a reassuring tone. Dad grabbed the rifle with ease and precision, into his shoulder, head tilted to the left, left eye closed. Ping!

"Bullseye!"

The old Carlton Draught beer can he had been saving flipped in the air and rolled and rattled its way to the edge of the garage.

"Wow, Dad, you are good," I said.

"You would hope so, mate, I didn't fight in that fucking war for nothing," he replied.

"Since you did so well today getting me the silencer, I have a present for ya," Dad said, handing me a Veterans Pass to get across the harbour bridge. I looked at the little card that would save me a few bucks. K.HILL. Expiry date 31/12/1999. I had three days left to use it.

"All you have to do is flash it; no one will check it," he assured me.

* * *

Two days later, I visited Mum and took her to her usual spot, the Balgowlah RSL Club. She liked it there because there was a salad bar, and she could pile her plate full of lettuce leaves, and a few other items - nothing with too many carbs, plus two generous glasses of the house white wine. I followed suit with a small rice salad on top, not wanting to appear gluttonous. We sat in the corner against the wall, Mum's favourite spot, hidden from the lunchtime crowd.

"Oh my god," Mum said in absolute disgust.

"What, Mum?"

"Look at the size of that woman over there, she is enormous!"

"Yeah, she is pretty big," I replied and sipped my wine.

I pushed my rice salad to the side. I no longer felt like it. After a quick lunch, I drove Mum home and headed back across the Sydney Harbour Bridge.

Mmm, maybe I will flash the card that Dad gave me...

I stopped and showed the toll booth operator my pass, but the book gate didn't open.

The toll booth operator scrutinised the card closely.

"What is your name?" he asked with a thick Indian accent.

"Kerry Hill," I nervously replied.

"This is a veteran's pass," the toll booth operator said. He took the pass and informed me that he would have to report it. He let me through the boom gate.

Fuck, Dad is going to kill me!

Dad invited me over for a beer that afternoon. As usual, I arrived with a six-pack of Carlton Draught. Dad looked like he had already had a few by the time I arrived.

"Matey, give us a hug," he said. I awkwardly embraced

his tall, large frame as I stepped on my tippy toes to kiss his hairy cheek. Alice was cooking dinner as usual.

"How is your mother? I miss her, you know… she was a good woman," he said.

"We all make mistakes, Dad," I said.

"Hey, did you use your pass I gave you?" Dad asked.

"Well, yeah, except the guy at the booth asked me my name and took it off me. He is going to report it to the police," I said.

"What the fuck, how could you be so stupid? What did he look like?" Dad yelled.

"He was an Indian man, that's all I know," I said defensively.

"That fucking rag head, they fucking come here to this country, like fucking heroes at the toll booth," he ranted.

"It's ok, Dad. It expires in two days anyway," I said.

"I fuckin' fought that war, what for? So that these rag heads can come into the country? Fuck that! Get us another beer. Fuck them," he mumbled under his breath as I walked away.

10

Cops Off Chops

I checked the Sydney Star Observer for the latest gay news and events, as well as LOTL (Lesbians On The Loose). There was a party at the Burdekin Hotel on Saturday night. I was rostered to work the night shift. Everyone was going, including Josh and Lynn. I called in sick to work, headed out for a run, and made sure to eat only half a sandwich all day, so I could look slim for it. I started making some calls.

"Hey Josh, can Charlie and Elizabeth come tonight?" That was code for cocaine and Eckys.

"Sure, darl, leave it with me," he said. Five hours later, we met at the hotel. Josh was at the bar, waiting with two beers: one for me and one for him.

"Did you get it?" I asked anxiously.

"Of course, darl," Josh responded in his calm manner, hands open with a huge smile, making his dimples indent in his smoothly shaved cheeks.

"Come to the toilet with me; the girls' toilet," he said. Inside the cubicle, Josh pulled out his NAB credit card and racked up two lines of coke on top of the stainless-steel toilet roll dispenser. Snort, sniff, and boom. Josh turned the water on at the hand basin area, cupped his hand, filled it with water and snorted it.

"This will help, darl, it's a bit gluggy. It's too humid," he explained.

Back at the bar, we threw down our beers, and I waited with excitement for Lynn to arrive. Lots of boys started to walk through the door, and Josh began to examine each specimen. One in particular caught his eye: shaved head, big muscles, tight blue jeans, and a white muscle tee. Josh's eyes went straight to his groin. He shouldered me.

"Oh my god, look at that!"

"Off you go, I'll wait here for Lynn."

This was the usual scene, and yet he always came back after an hour or so. I trusted him; he had my back, and I had his.

I met many people and got deeply into partying, drugs, and dancing. I never wanted to go home. I tried various drugs like MDA, ecstasy, amphetamines, cocaine, ketamine, marijuana, LSD and Meow Meow. I avoided heroin despite its presence in other drugs. I used multiple methods to consume them. Recovery parties became a dress-up party at a friend's house where we would tip what we had left over, usually a mix of MDA, speed, coke and 'K' (Ketamine) crushed up and snorted. Getting to sleep two days later was a mix of the come-down drugs: Valium, Normison, Temazepam, Xanax, Stilnox; whatever I could get my hands on. My other life, the one where I was a mother to a mother, or a cop, or trying to get Dad's approval, was swept aside in a desperate desire to fit in, be seen and escape. Nothing filled my insatiable desire to be loved, 'Like some kind of lonely clown,' as the band The Carpenters would sing.

Lynn moved back to Canada after I cheated on her. I was running again to find the one who loved me more. I had a few lovers after that, and then I met Eleni. Nobody would ever say a bad word about Eleni; she was just one of those lovable people. She exuded warmth and affection. I would often watch in awe as she sat on people's laps at dance parties and chatted for hours. She was tiny, a Greek woman in height and frame. I was too busy avoiding conversations and dancing on the podium to engage properly in a relationship. The drugs elevated my ego, and I was not interested in connection unless it was sexual.

Eleni and I were girlfriends for three years. The usual partying continued, and in the meantime, I met another party cop on the dance floor. Jules was outspoken, the sort of person you could rely on.. She was also very tall, encouraging and influential with a striking appearance.

I introduced Toni to Jules, and we all became great friends. I shared my 30th birthday with Eleni, Toni and Jules, plus a large handful of other friends I had made over the years. I dressed up as Cocaine Carol.

Carol was dressed in Eleni's tight-fitting lime green dress with a wide collar that flared into a miniskirt. Carol was the epitome of Jane Jetson from the "Jetsons" comical TV series. Jane was a space-aged housewife who knew how to run a household, a supportive mother to her children, and a wife to George.

Carol was eager to give her guests a welcome gift.

It was 4pm and the doorbell rang. The first guest had arrived: Jules. Cocaine Carol walked gently to the door in her dress three sizes too small, with a platter of white lines.

"Welcome! Wanna line?" I asked.

"Of course!" Jules said as she placed the rolled-up note in her nostril and sniffed enthusiastically. The next guest was Toni.

"Line?" I asked.

"Seriously, of course!" Another hoover took the plate.

Within an hour, the guests started to arrive. Carol was busy at the door, and everyone was high, drinking and mingling. I had a surprise that evening. I'd been rehearsing the dance routine to Kylie Minogue's version of "I can't get you out of my head."

Once everyone was well lubricated and their noses powdered, including Carol, the music began. I lost the Jetsons outfit and got ready for my performance.

Twenty or so people were seated in the backyard of the "Chiswick", a charming cottage where Eleni lived with her flatmate, Rachel. The music started. I came out standing on the top steps, eyes black, now in a new, shimmering, tight dress. The audience was ready. I moved my body from side to side, getting down low, playing to the crowd, taking off my top, dancing topless like an amateur at a gentleman's club, waiting for the note to be tucked down my pants with the eye of the wanting.

After everyone left, Rachel and I ended up in the sunroom, drinking wine and singing, 'It's time for you to stop all your sobbing,' by The Pretenders.

Eleni and I worked well in an avoidance kind of way, meaning that we avoided anything too personal or controversial. Eleni would turn a blind eye to my early morning notes once she fell asleep:

'Sleep well, I'm going out. I'll see you in a few hours. 7am. Xxx.'

After three years, our relationship ended; however, we remain very good friends to this day.

11

Dress Rehearse Tragedy

By my early 30s, Mum was severely depressed and very thin. I would take her and my grandmother to the Balgowlah RSL Club every week. Dad and I were working on past issues. I accepted his partner, Alice, though I wasn't sure if I emotionally trusted her. I believed Dad felt guilty for leaving Mum. I arranged a meeting for the three of us.

I picked Dad up from his home in Bronte, Sydney. Dad was waiting outside with a new look. I hadn't seen him in months. His hair was tied back in a ponytail, a longish beard, and a dark brown leather vest handsomely fit his masculine physique. He spun around.

"What do you reckon?" he asked.

On the back of the leather vest was a black circular

badge. The top read "VETERANS" in yellow embroidery, the side read "MC", and the bottom read "AUSTRALIA". In the centre was a skeleton's face wearing a slouched cap. Dad had just started his chapter with the Vietnam Veterans MC club.

"I bought a new bike, but don't tell your mother she hates them. Wanna have a look, Matey?"

He took me inside the garage; Alice was at work. A brand-new maroon coloured Dyna Wide Glide Harley-Davidson shone in all its glory. The handlebars were high and wide, adorned with symbols of war and touches of Dad. Many Vietnam Vets returned home traumatised and unrecognised, trusting only their 'Brothers in Arms'. Dad started the bike; its roar brought a smile of pride and belonging to his face. His soul was alive.

As Dad and I walked outside onto the busy footpath, a cyclist swerved sharply to avoid a collision with us.

"If you ride your bike past my house one more fucking time, I swear I'll fucking shoot you!" Dad yelled.

"Come on, Dad, let it go," I said.

"I'm sick to death of these fucking yuppies that live in this place," he said, jaw clenched and fists tight.

We jumped in what was now my black Nissan Pulsar, Peggy. I drove so Dad could have a few drinks. Over the

Sydney Harbour Bridge, we headed into the North Shore. A short time later, we walked into the famous Oaks Hotel. It's called the Oaks because there is a massive oak tree in the middle of the beer garden, which is draped in fairy lights, ready to expose the symbolic hardwood tree with unusually lobed-edged leaves, and a huge supportive trunk.

It was noon, and I liked to leave at least thirty minutes early to get a table, but then again, so did Mum. Dad and I walked in through the beer garden. I saw Mum sitting at the top of the stairs overlooking the beer garden in the smoking area. Mum was dressed smartly, in a pale blue, yet baggy linen shirt and a pair of navy blue pants, her hair done and makeup on; the usual appearance. Since Mum and I had the same fear about getting a spot, she already had a glass of wine in her hand. Dad and Mum hadn't seen each other for many months. The three of us sat down as if it were old times, and a few drinks helped lubricate the awkward atmosphere.

"Mate, can you grab me and your mother a drink?" he asked as he handed me a $10 note.

"Don't forget the change," he said with a serious smirk on his face. Dad liked to pile his coins on the table as a restriction on his spending for the day. I obligingly walked to the bar for a round of drinks: a schooner of Carlton for Dad and two glasses of house wine for Mum and me.

As I sat down, the attention turned to me.

"So, Shelley, how are you liking the cops?" Dad asked.

"Mm, it's pretty good. I have met some great people and we have drinks after work some days, plus the Christmas party is coming up at the local army barracks, and they give us half price drinks," I said.

Mum was silent, as she nervously grabbed her glass of wine and drew it to her mouth. I noticed the veins in her elegant hands were prominent, more than normal. Her arms were so thin, almost spindly, like the mosquito that buzzed around me at Centennial Park when Dad and I were catching tortoises. Dad seemed nervous, and although I had spent time with Dad a few months ago, he asked a random question.

"Do they let you out in the police truck?"

My frown line pressed intensely together.

"Yes, Dad, and sometimes two females might go out on patrol. You know, maybe this might happen in the Fireys one day!" I gritted my teeth.

"And are you on the take?"

"No, Dad, I'm not taking things from crims or stealing from a deceased person's home."

Dads raised his eyebrows, surprised.

"I'm not like you, Dad!" I said with a serious tone.

"Mate, remember what I told you, you don't get something for nothing, and the cops are always on the take. I've seen it," he replied confidently.

"I have to go to the bathroom," Mum said. The toilets were a few steps down and to the left. She pushed her tiny body with her frail hands off the chair, stumbled to the left and then to the right. I watched as her head hit the pavement. Crack! She had fallen down the stairs. I rushed down, and she was not moving. Patrons and staff rushed over.

"Someone call 000!" I yelled.

I kneeled down beside her, and Dad stood over her body.

She is unconscious, but not a lot of blood for such a fall.

"It's ok, Mum," I said, my voice quivering.

Within minutes, paramedics arrived and Mum was taken out on a stretcher as sirens wailed in the distance. Dad turned to me.

"Mate, you'd better go and look after your mother," he said.

"I'll take you home first, Dad."

I don't know what to do. There is no blood, but how will Dad get home?

I couldn't think straight. I drove frantically across the harbour bridge back to Dad's house.

About an hour later, I arrived at Royal North Shore Hospital. Mum had just come back from X-rays. Doctors were waiting, waiting for someone to answer heaps of questions.

Why didn't I just go straight to Royal North Shore Hospital instead of taking Dad home?

"So, Shelley, are you the main support person for your mum?" the Doctor asked.

"Yes, well, and her mum, but she is in her eighties," I replied.

"What is your mother's date of birth?' he asked.

"28 January, 1945," I said.

"Your mother is very thin, emaciated in fact."

"Yes, she has anorexia," I replied.

"What else can you tell me about your mother?"

"She has Lupus, heart disease, she has had a stroke, and she smokes a packet of cigarettes a day and drinks a 4-litre cask of wine a week," I said.

"Do you know if she takes any medication?" he asked.

"Yes, antidepressants, blood thinners, and Valium."

"Does she work?" he asked.

"No, she is on a disability pension."

The ICU room was notably cold, and the hospital showed signs of needing repair. The smell was pervasive and uncomfortable. The metal curtain rings scraped against the rail as the blue curtains were drawn. My mother's white hospital gown sat above her knee cap. Her large knees were attached to pale skeletal legs, and a thick hospital bandage surrounded her head with blood and fluid slightly oozing through the fabric. Doctors and nurses shuffled around the bed, taking observations, monitoring the machine and looking for signs of agitation. The smell of the hospital was a memory akin to a dead body, one that never left the olfactory senses.

"Ok, let's get Joy into surgery, now!" he said in a loud, assertive voice to his team.

"Shelley, if something like this happens again, you must come straight away. Your mum has a subarachnoid haemorrhage, a subdural hematoma and multiple contusions. Basically, she has a severe bleed to her brain, and we are going to do a craniotomy and get a drain in there to drain the blood; otherwise, she will die."

I called Gran and she ordered a taxi.

**

Gran arrived at the hospital; her clothing was tidy, plain-faced, with no signs of distress.

"Hello, Dear," she said as she sat down. Hours passed with intensity as we waited in the hard, green plastic chairs for any sign of news from the doctors. Unspoken words drifted in and out between us. Troubling thoughts interfered with my food pyramid.

I ate muesli with yoghurt, two cups of coffee with full cream milk. I hope Mum is ok? I better not show concern to Gran, then one piece of toast, why didn't I come straight to the hospital after she fell, I–

My chain of thought was broken by a doctor coming straight toward us. His face looked soft. A slight frown lined his face. He knelt down.

"Your mother is very lucky; she has pulled through, but it is not over yet. We have to keep her under observation; she is very frail, and there is a lot of pressure on her body to fight the invasive surgery," he said in a gentle and direct voice.

Gran and I sat in peak hour traffic back to Manly to her one-bedroom unit. She was as stoic as they come, fiercely independent, and well-liked. She showed love in a practical way; there wasn't enough time for affection coming from a family of nine in 1901 when horse and cart were the only means of transport. Mum wanted to please her mother and grasped at the need for approval just like a newborn grabs the bottle in a failed attempt to connect, hands not strong enough to ensure the grip required.

"I just don't understand why Joy doesn't eat?" Gran said in disbelief.

"She doesn't have a healthy relationship with herself, and it seems to have gotten worse since Dad left," I said with hesitation.

"She should never have married that man; he was no good for her," Gran said.

She bore a resemblance to the Queen of England, as I observed the brooch on her blue, scooped-neck blouse and her tightly permed grey hair, sprayed liberally with Taft hairspray.

"Bye, Dear," she said as she got out of the car. "Let me know if you hear any news."

"Will do, Gran," I said. We parted ways, and I made the trek home across the city bumper to bumper.

I ate half a bowl of salad today with half a baguette. I ate one bowl of salad today with half a baguette.

I watched the brake lights of the car in front flash on and off.

Back home, I made my way upstairs to my unit, which was situated above a Thai restaurant, on a main road in Coogee. The smell of cooking oil filled my senses, as did the sound of the wok scraping sharply across the hotplate. I called work and was approved for Family and Community Service Leave to care for Mum. It would be a long recovery, given that Mum weighed under thirty-five kilograms.

I poured myself a glass of cold, crisp white wine, and all I could hear was the sound of my mother's skull hitting the pavement. I placed my hands around my face and just cried.

Perhaps this is Mum's time, maybe this is the end? How will she survive this, and what if her brain can't function, what if she is a vegetable?

I began to write Mum's eulogy. I was prepared for death, prepared for loss, prepared for grief. I armoured up, shoulders back and took a big sip of my wine. The condensation hugged the crystal exterior, and little beads of water fell slowly down the stem. My tears made their way onto the page.

"There are not enough words to describe Mum, she was…"

I can't write anymore. I don't want to feel this anymore.

I skulled my wine and turned out the lights to the sound of laughter and loud voices talking over pad thai and crying tiger.

After a few weeks, I returned to work and was assigned to Lakemba to hand out tickets on trains. It was easier than general policing, and I did well. This job restored my faith in the police culture. I worked with great colleagues who were misfits like me in the NSW Police Force. Biff, my boss, advocated for me to join the Sydney Water Police, a prestigious role where pulling bodies from the water became routine.

I visited Mum as much as I could, often collecting Gran from Manly and driving her home. Mum was mostly delusional and talking rubbish, with the oozing bandage wrapped around her head

***

About six weeks after the accident, I went to visit. Mum was upright in bed, in a single room. The doctor approached me.

"Your mother is doing well, and we are going to transfer her to the Brain Injury Unit for a prolonged recovery," he said.

That is where Mum spent the next six months. At fifty-seven years of age, she needed aid for walking, self-care, and mental health. Significant gains were made in improving her physical fitness and functional abilities, and she also gained 18.7 kilograms. She weighed 52.6kg on discharge. However, her theme of depression and self-worthlessness remained. I had returned to work, but my head was just not in the job, so I did what I knew best: made sure I looked after Mum and Gran and numbed the rest with alcohol and drugs. The emptiness inside and the search for a new partner to fill the void led me to Amy, yet I was hiding a secret.

12

Culpam Poena Premit Comes (Punishment swiftly follows crime)

Amy and I met through mutual friends and had been together for months. Amy was Swedish, caring, and had a three-year-old son. Our relationship was stable and calm, without excess partying. In the beginning, I began to recognise my emotionally unavailable parents, and this sense of abandonment was triggered every time I saw Amy and her son cuddled on the couch. I would isolate myself and sit on the floor in a childlike sulky tantrum, even though there was plenty of room for me.

Why is he allowed junk food? His room is untidy and he doesn't have to set the table.

I tried to enforce the rules my mother instilled in me, yet this just left me angry and needy, and of course, Amy's number one priority was her child. I was glued to perfectionism, and drinking took the edge off, whilst authenticity and connection prevailed.

It wasn't long into our relationship before Toni, Jules, and I were tipped off that we were under investigation for taking drugs. By this stage I was living with Toni, and we were informed that our 2-bedroom unit was bugged and the landline tapped.

Toni and Jules worked in different areas of the police, but we always caught up, either at the regular nightclub, or drinks and parties at friends' houses. I decided to let Amy know what was going on, so we met down at Coogee Beach for a walk one day.

"Hey, I've got something I need to tell you," I said.

Amy was matter-of-fact in her approach to life.

"What is it?"

"Well, I think I'm in trouble. Well, not just me, Toni and Jules too. We got a tip-off that we are being investigated for taking drugs."

"Ok, you know what you've been doing is wrong, so I guess you will have to pay the consequence."

"Yeah, I know," I said, brushing Amy's comment to the side.

"Anyway, I've got to tell two of my friends tomorrow

night, will you come with me?"

Amy was happy to come and support me, so we grabbed a coffee and took in the glimmer of the ocean, sitting in silence.

***

It was a cold Monday night in Sydney. Amy and I walked into a warm, dimly lit wine bar in Potts Point to sit in a green leather booth. We huddled together waiting. Liz and Meg arrived a few minutes later. I introduced Amy, and we all ordered a round of cocktails to start.

Liz and Meg were my 'party' friends. Amy wasn't really into the 'scene' and didn't drink. The energy was awkward, and the atmosphere of the restaurant felt eerie.

Is it just me?

Anxiously, I got straight to the point.

"I'm just letting you guys know I am under investigation, and I have had a tip-off from another cop that my landline is tapped and my house is bugged," I said. Paranoia struck like the deadly brown snake, head reared, aggressive and ready to fight the moment I told my party friends the news.

"What the actual fuck! What do you mean?" cried Liz, in a high-pitched tone. "Does that mean we are in trouble, too?"

Drama escalated as the wine was gulped down.

"Shelley, you won't be able to come to the party next weekend, it's too risky," said Meg.

Amy sat quiet. The waiter approached our table.

"Is there someone here called Shelley?" he asked with curiosity.

"Yes, that's me," I said, panicked.

"You have a call from someone called Eleni," he said.

Liz and Meg had met Eleni when we were dating. My heart beating hard, I nervously pulled the bottom of my t-shirt away from my body at least four times as I walked to the chunky green telephone, with the slightly twisted cord.

"Hello?" I said quietly.

"It's me," Eleni said. I recognised her voice instantly.

"Get out of the restaurant now!" she said desperately. "Amy is a spy!"

What?!

My hands trembled as I placed the receiver down and walked back to the table. Everyone was staring at me intensely.

"Who was that?!" pleaded Meg. I was not sure how to respond to what I'd just heard. Six eyes stared at me.

"That was Eleni, she reckons Amy is a spy!" I said, finally finding my voice.

Eleni was always overprotective; where did she get this information from?

Liz and Meg had told Eleni they were meeting Amy tonight. All heads turned to Amy, including mine.

Amy doesn't work; she is self-funded from her ex, the father of her son... Could it be true?

I could see Amy tensing up, folding her arms with little expression on her face.

"Maybe I should just leave?" she said finally.

"No, no. This is getting out of control, let's just calm down," I said.

We ordered more drinks and tried to laugh it off.

"Shelley, you need to leave the country... NOW!" Liz said a short while later in a drunken slur.

"What! This is ridiculous!" I replied.

My friends were in a drunken frenzy. Amy stormed out. Meg, Liz and I grabbed the bill and piled into a taxi, back to my place. I knocked softly on the door of the apartment. It was about 9pm, and Toni slowly opened our door. Liz placed her right index finger to her lips.

"Shush, get Shelley's passport now," she said urgently. "She needs to leave the country tonight!"

"That is the most insane thing I have heard yet," said Toni.

"Guys, go home. Shelley is not leaving the country."

I called Amy as soon as they left.

"I'm sorry about tonight," I said.

"That was too much, and by the way, I am not a spy.

Plus, I have a son to look after," she said in response.

Six months later, things really started heating up, and the tip-offs became more frequent. I handed in my resignation on November 1, 2003, after thirteen years of employment with the NSW Police. It was the perfect push to get out. I handed in my badge with a deep sense of relief, and Amy and I continued our relationship.

A few days later, there was a knock at my front door. I looked through the peephole and saw two uniformed male cops. I nervously opened the door.

"Are you Shelley Hill?" one of them asked in a profoundly serious tone.

"Yes," I replied.

"Then this is for you," he said and handed me a nine-page document.

The document was a summons to give evidence at the Police Integrity Commission, in five days' time. The hearing was a public event, and notice of it was also published in a major newspaper on the same day. Toni and Jules received the same document that day.

I still wondered if Amy was really a spy, like my friends suggested. We never argued about it; it was just the elephant in the room. We really loved each other, and I assumed it was all high drama. My time had come as I got dressed in a black suit, ready for court. Amy drove Toni, Jules and me to the courtroom on St James Street in Sydney.

"Good luck, girls," she said as we hopped out of her car. My hands shook, and a deep sense of shame engulfed me.

What a mess. I've really fucked up.

The revolving doors of the chambers led me to the reality of my punishment.

The courtroom was crowded with people of various ages and professions, drawn in by extensive newspaper coverage of the controversial case. Conversations fell silent as officials arrived, signalling the start of the proceedings. Anticipation filled the room. I tried to recite my food pyramid, but realised all I'd had was one coffee. A large TV screen displayed recorded conversations between the police involved and drug suppliers investigated over the past year.

I took my seat, ready for questioning. I admitted to taking drugs despite being a police officer and obtaining illegal substances from a friend who was a supplier. I confirmed to counsel that in 1998, I passed a drug test but had taken drugs three to four days prior. I admitted to calling in sick due to drug use on many occasions over seven years. Knowing my drug use was recreational and that I did not supply drugs, I answered my final question honestly.

"So Senior Constable Hill, why is it that you took

drugs while in the police?" I was asked.

"It's part of my lifestyle and I enjoy it," I said.

It was the truth, and the verdict was no criminal conviction. I breathed a sigh of relief.

It was a gruelling day, and we knew the press were waiting out the front, ready to take some photos, so Toni suggested we try and sneak out the back to avoid further scrutiny.

"Let's get a drink," I said, and the three of us scurried to the nearest pub with a television. A few beers in, and the 6 o'clock news came on. Pauline Hanson had taken the first headline. Next was "Three Police Admit Long-Term Drug Habits." Our full names were plastered across the screen.

What will my parents think?

They had no idea. I didn't have to think for long; it was only minutes later that the phone calls started coming.

"I can't believe you are a drug addict!" Mum cried, sobbing down the phone. The shame I had brought to my family was unbearable.

Dad's anger was palpable.

"I just saw your name on the TV, what the fuck?" he demanded.

"It is not as bad as it looks, Dad. I will call you tomorrow," I cried.

Dad's had a few. It is so not worth the argument.

I was ostracised from the family and left the police force with a Diploma of Shameful Behaviour. I felt disconnected from myself and others. I was numb, angry, and yearning for something different.

13

Your life Is As Good As Your Mindset

Though Amy was never a spy, our relationship fell apart, mostly because I was on the prowl again. Toni and I moved out, and I started partying again, eventually living alone and struggling to pay rent. Mum was living independently in the same unit block as Gran, and she never saw Dad again after her fall. On one of my nights out, I was introduced to a woman called Lynn, who was a fit-looking woman from the "Valleys" in Wales. Her accent was so thick I had trouble understanding her.

I started working for Lynne and I loved it. Her Frida Kahlo eyebrows and blokey nature made work easy. If you fucked up, you got told to fuck off. There would be a bit of a tantrum, then it would be back to normal. She was tough, yet fair. I was earning $150 a day. Long, exhausting days, shovelling bricks, digging trenches, plasterboarding walls, mainly in the inner west of Sydney. 7am start until 4pm or when Lynne had had enough. She would work all night if she could. Her team were mainly women, including an accredited female carpenter and a female apprentice. I did this for four years, and it was my favourite job to date. I loved the physicality of the job, yet I knew I couldn't sustain this type of physical work, along with the pay. I had some partners at this time, the usual lineup for a serial monogamist like me: two years, six months, three years. I was never quite ready, couldn't commit. Generally, nothing much had changed - until one day it did.

* * *

In 2007, I was single and enjoying a hot summer day. I walked to my favourite ocean pool, paid twenty cents, and found my spot on a flat rock away from crowds. There was a tiny stagnant rock pool nearby, and I swatted away mosquitoes until I applied coconut oil. At 9am, before the masses arrived, I felt joy as I watched the sea sparkle. Then, I climbed over rocks to dive into the ocean pool. The water invigorated my body, and I stopped to say three things to myself that I was grateful for. I liked to make it simple.

One. I have a roof over my head. Two. I'm blessed to submerge my body in this salty and healing water. Three. I have beautiful people and guides who surround me.

This location was revered as a sacred spot for Indigenous women, offering a sense of calm. I had begun a search for something deeper and enrolled in a Metaphysics course. I'd become interested in Shamanism, Numerology, spirit guides, anything esoteric, and that was just the beginning.

That afternoon, Toni and I caught up, and she suggested that we go and see a band in the Blue Mountains in a week's time.

"Great, I'll grab a bottle of bubbles," I offered.

"You can't bring alcohol," Toni replied.

"What do you mean?" I said, surprised.

"It's an alcohol free event."

"Okay then," I said slowly, feeling a little reluctant to go.

I'm not sure how fun this will be, but I don't want to let her down.

One week later, Toni and I drove through a large set of gates that took us onto a gravelled road. Huge trees lined the way to a rustic wooden sign, "Brahma Kumaris Centre For Spiritual Learning."

We arrived at a grassed area with rugs laid out. As dusk approached, fairy lights sparkled behind the band we were about to see. A woman sat with a cello between her legs, joined by others ready to play their instruments. The band was called 'Bliss,' there to promote their new album 'One Hundred Thousand Angels'.

Grounded on the grass, I sat with an open mind. The lead female vocalist had a soft, clear voice. The lyrics profoundly resonated with me, particularly phrases such as: 'Let me walk you through your life, there's a hundred thousand angels by your side.' I departed that evening, experiencing a blend of euphoria and sorrow; the words evoked a range of emotions, tapping into my inner darkness.

My spiritual curiosity had been ignited, and I was scared, yet I decided to embark on a Raja Yoga meditation weekend course at the Brahma Kumaris Centre. I had only ever seen the grassy area where Bliss had played. As I drove to the entrance of the main building, it felt familiar. Like a motel, with little doors to the left. The dark green and cream exterior led to a cozy room with a warm fireplace, crackling wood, and two chequered lounges facing each other. I was taken out of my memory with a soft voice, "Welcome to the Brahma Kumaris Centre. There is a book over there, could you please sign in?" It was a donation-only system, and you could also help in the kitchen to prep for the vegetarian meals or clean up afterwards. This is where I would learn the basics of Raja Yoga meditation.

I walked to my room. A dark green wooden door led me into the same colonial-themed interior. Two single beds with brown and green chequered bedspreads, a dark green valance surrounded the base of the bed, neatly ironed. The interior walls were red brick. I quickly turned on my Dimplex heater and sat on the edge of the bed. At 4:45 pm, I proceeded to the main room, a spacious and aesthetically pleasing area adorned with a large black-and-white photograph of Brahma Baba, an elderly man, displayed prominently on the wall above a stage. The environment was comforting and cozy. My teacher sat on a stage dressed in white; she exuded warmth, and her energy was grounded and soft. I prepared to commence my first session. Raja Yoga is an open-eye meditation resulting in a deep connection to the soul, and it teaches us to observe life and to respond with love. After learning about the concept of reincarnation, which they call the Wheel of Life, Karma, and the basic notion of self-transformation, I was eager to sit in silence, yet negative thoughts about myself consumed my attempt at peace.

Fuck, I have made so many mistakes in my life, I've damaged my career, and I've hurt people deeply.

I wiped the tears from my eyes and stared at a point on the wall until I could feel my body relax. Intrusive thoughts prevailed, yet I tried to have a little compassion for myself. The next day was filled with more meditation and learning; this time, I brought my journal. An older man, a palliative care Doctor who practised Raja Yoga, entered the room and I absorbed his words, his wisdom and love. I scratched some of the things he said as I admired his gentle, soothing voice.

"When you think someone is amazing, you are actually looking for that quality within yourself and realising your true potential."

"Serve the world from who I am, rather than who I should be."

"I can be in chaos yet detach and remain peaceful."

"The ego is a set of false beliefs. Love is the destruction of the ego."

To my astonishment, I successfully participated throughout the entire weekend, engaging in learning, listening, and experiencing meditation. It was a humbling experience.

Back home, I meditated most days. I felt less anxious, yet I was recognising my old triggers and reality; it felt like one foot in, one foot out. A few months later, I noticed the Brahma Kumaris Centre was holding a workshop. It was run by Judith Shepherd-Pemell, a female psychotherapist committed to the practice of Raja Yoga Meditation, exclusive to the Brahma Kumaris Centre. The workshop was geared towards people with addictions. I signed up.

I drove to the Blue Mountains, stopped on my way and popped into a pub for a glass of wine.

I'm not an addict, I'm simply curious about the workshop.

Driving in, I felt a sense of déjà vu again. Anxiety set in as my heart pounded. After signing in and getting my room key, I could have killed for another glass of wine. I walked to my room, my mind racing.

Should I just sneak out and leave? This is a stupid idea. I had a glass of wine before I came. I am an imposter.

Something made me stay. I waited until 4.45pm, and then walked to the main hall for the 5pm introduction session. I was terrified.

Chairs were set up in a circle. I introduced myself to the facilitator, Judy. I nervously chose a chair. I was the first to arrive. A tall, slender, black woman walked in; she had a presence about her, elegant and stunningly beautiful. She took a seat next to me.

"Hey, I'm Vic," she said with a posh English accent.

It turned out Vic had been clean and sober for two years. Over the next four days, we shared stories, ate meals together, and meditated every morning. One of the most challenging exercises was walking around the room and stopping to gaze into someone's eyes for a full minute whenever Judy rang her bell. On the second round, I stopped in front of a woman who must have been twenty years older than me; her gaze was soft and secure.

I could not hold back my tears; I felt as if we had been in a past life together. I went back to my room and cried, a happy-sad sort of cry. Within the last twenty-four hours, I felt a connection with others, excited, and this place held me tight. On the last night, when I was getting ready for bed, I suddenly remembered why this place held such a memory.

I had visited some years back when it was operating under a different name, "Where Waters Meet." I had been with Mum and Gran after Mum had just been discharged from the psychiatric unit. Gran and I decided to take her away to cheer her up. The enormity of her suicide attempt and diagnosis of anorexia came flashing to my mind as I sat on the floor of my room and sobbed, a release of deep sadness.

Attending the weekend workshop did not flick a switch within to suddenly start waking up clean and sober, but it certainly gave me a connection to others, a connection to spirit and a deeper connection to myself. On the last day, Vic turned to me.

"I think you should meet a friend of mine in Sydney, she is gay, you would get along, she is really cool," she said.

"Yeah, maybe," I said. After all, I had been single for six months. Vic and I swapped numbers. A week later, back home in Sydney, I met Nadia, a backpacker from

Bournemouth, England. A Moroccan father, with dark hair and eyes wide apart, charming, skinny, and in recovery. A few dates, and her street-smart skills came out. She had left home in her teenage years and been homeless in Spain. She was living in and out of hostels in Sydney when I met her. She had a very encouraging nature, which pushed me to be more self-confident, and eventually led me to let her move in. My friends were concerned and thought I was being taken advantage of. They nicknamed her BP, short for backpacker. I was more curious about her lifestyle. She practised Buddhism daily, reciting prayers every morning and attending the Buddhist Centre at Bondi Junction weekly to study Kadampa Buddhism.

"Why don't you come one Thursday night with me?" she said.

"Why not," I replied. I was not drinking too much then, given that she was in recovery and I was trying to make a good impression.

Thursday night came around, and I managed to get a park in busy Bondi Junction. I walked a few blocks to the tall, aging and tired building. I noticed the paint was peeling and the wrought iron balustrade was rusting. It was located on a noisy and busy road, the traffic jammed at the lights outside, and pedestrians scurried to catch the bus down to Bondi Beach. The façade did not deter me as

I walked in and up a flight of stairs to my left. The terraced house was filled with soft lighting, fruits, and flowers, and had a warm energy. A large golden statue of a Buddha sat peacefully amidst little ceramic cups and gold elephants. I was nervous. Nadia knew everyone, including the monks. It felt like a false scenario for me, pretending and trying to be something different; the imposter was back, and again, something made me stay.

I took my seat among other curious students in an uncomfortable plastic chair, eager to hear what the Buddhist teacher had to share. We all sat still as Jinpa walked into the room. His voice was soft and his blue eyes sparkled. I was mesmerised. He had a well-shaped, shaved head and wore a red and golden robe. As Jinpa sat down on his chair on a stage, surrounded by elephant statues, flowers and offerings, we all took hold of our booklet and sang along to the Liberating Prayer, recited at the start of any learning session. As I partially closed my eyes, ready for mediation, my mind was busy.

What will I have for dinner? Is everyone else struggling? Maybe this is not my thing.

I tried to resist my consuming thoughts and go back to my breath. Jinpa announced that the lesson tonight would be about self-grasping and the faults of anger. I had purchased a green leather-bound notebook.

He began to speak, calmly and deliberately, and

something in me stilled. I found myself scribbling down his words like they were lifelines.

He was paraphrasing from Velnerable Geshe Kelsang Gyatso's *How to Solve Our Human Problems*, though I didn't know that at the time. All I knew was that his words hit like truth.

"Self-grasping is the principal cause of our suffering. It destroys our inner peace. Our enemies aren't out there. Nothing external causes us happiness or suffering. Nothing is permanent - only our ignorance thinks it is."

That sentence cracked something open in me. I'd spent years believing it was the people or the circumstances outside me that were the problem. But what if… it wasn't?

He kept going:

"Anger and jealousy are elaborate fantasies."

"Samsara is the prison of our own perception."

"We don't like being forced into situations we don't choose, but we always have a choice in how we respond."

I felt exposed. Seen. Called in and called out, all at once. He spoke of choice in the way we react to difficult situations. When we can't get what we want, we get unhappy. He explained that it was our attachment that could cause us to get angry. We get attached to how things 'should be' and just need to learn new ways of reacting. These concepts cracked me open. Parts of me wanted to argue, to make an exception for my story, my pain, my past. But deep down, I knew I had been trapped in the prison of my own perceptions.

The following Thursday, with an eager desire to learn, I took my seat, yet this time it was Dae, a female monk, leading the class. She had a shaved head, a strong presence and the same gentle voice. The lesson was on "Affectionate Love/Compassion". I couldn't write quick enough as her words fell onto my page.

I wrote the teachings and words of wisdom down with inspiration and excitement raging through my body as Dae spoke.

"We can ripen our karmic connection to all living beings by developing love for all living beings, a universal love. All of us are similar and share so much; we are one family wishing to be free from suffering. The more we generate love for others, the more they appear beautiful. Focus on people's good qualities," she said.

What I was learning was that from the Buddhist perspective, we could control our minds and make a choice about how we reacted or responded to difficult situations. Pain didn't come from external conditions, eg, our boss, our partner, etc – it came from our mind.

After that night, something shifted in me. I started showing up every Thursday evening, eager to dive deeper into the teachings I'd been introduced to. What began as simple curiosity quickly turned into a weekly ritual, and soon after, I found myself meditating every single day. These moments of stillness and reflection began to peel back layers I didn't even realise I was carrying. Bit by bit, I was remembering who I was beneath the noise of life.

The teachings weren't just theoretical—they were deeply practical. I began seeing the world through a softer lens. I was reminded to treat all living beings with kindness, not just in theory, but in the tiny everyday moments that shape our relationships. I learned that when we choose to see the good in others, something magical happens—they begin to reflect that goodness back. I realised it was not about ignoring mine or someone else's flaws, but rather, choosing to focus on the light instead of the shadows.

One of the biggest revelations was realising how often we search externally for what already exists within us. That endless striving, that chasing, I realised had disconnected me from my own inner wisdom. I was realising if I turned inward with compassion and curiosity, I could come home to myself. It was through this lens that I began to understand forgiveness not as a one-time act, but as an ongoing process—one that could free me from the weight of what has been and create space for what could be.

I was coming to see that the way we show up in the world matters. Every act of love, every moment of acceptance, could become a kind of spiritual investment—fuel for the future version of myself I was creating. Perhaps most humbling of all, I was learning that we can't bypass pain. Healing isn't about avoidance; it's about courageously walking through the dark to find the light on the other side.

There was something deeply empowering about letting go of who I thought I should be and instead choosing to start to live from a place of truth. When I allowed things to unfold as they were—without trying to control or fix them—I was practising a new form of self-respect. Even something as simple as connecting to my breath became a powerful reminder of the present moment and its ability to soothe, anchor, and renew.

I was beginning to realise that trauma wouldn't just dissolve if I ignored it. It really was that clichéd saying: We can't go around it, and we certainly can't go under it. The only way out is through—and while that path wouldn't be easy, it is where real healing begins. Little did I realise then just how much I would need to rely on these teachings.

* * *

A year later, Nadia and I ended up in Singapore and sat with people from around the world to be blessed by Geshe Kelsang Gyatso, the head of Kadampa Buddhism. This was a big deal, and I felt incredibly privileged. After three years of dedication to the tradition, Jinpa gave me my own set of little ritual cups, and every morning I would recite the prayers written by Geshe. I purchased the book, "How to Solve Our Human Problems", and inside, my Buddhist teacher wrote:

"Dear Shelley, all happiness and suffering come from within the mind. May you develop the internal happiness that comes from a perfectly beautiful mind. Lots of love. K, Jinpa."

By this stage, Nadia had left me for a friend of mine. They were much more suited, and the practice of forgiveness and acceptance allowed me to heal from the rejection. I wished them both happiness every day, even though I didn't feel it at the time. I wanted my mind to be filled with compassion and love, not anger and resentment.

As I progressed further down this path, I sought healers such as kinesiologists, energetic healers, mediums, tarot readers and astrologers. I also pursued my own personal counselling as a therapeutic process. These new tools allowed me to accept and deal with what life was about to present with more tolerance, more love and less anger.

14

In For the Long Haul, 2007

I lost interest in the dance party scene and was happy being single, until one Sunday afternoon, my friends dragged me out to the Trademark Hotel, situated above the neon lights of the Coca-Cola sign in Kings Cross. I wasn't in the mood for large crowds, the usual DJs and the same faces from the last fifteen years in the clubs. I was 36 years old and was just starting to view life with a little more curiosity and depth. I was on a path of discovering who I was, and then I met Daniella, a tanned, muscular, attractive Brazilian woman. She was 28 years old, had long dark hair, smiling brown eyes and a smile so big, it was hard not to smile back.

She was there with a group of Brazilians that she had met in Australia, and hadn't been long in the country. Her English was poor, so we did a lot of head nodding, pretending we understood each other. I asked if I could have a cigarette.

"Oi, Ca, cigarro," she replied, putting her hand up in the air trying to get her friend's attention. I was introduced to her friend Carla. Her English was well executed and her style classy as she handed Daniella and me a cigarette each.

"Obrigada," said Daniella. I was feeling a little happier than when I first arrived. Daniella's energy was charming and engaging, forceful and passionate, and her kiss matched her intensity.

I left with my friends a few hours later, after exchanging numbers with Daniella. A week later, we started dating, and like most new relationships, it was fun and sexy. I was still attending my regular Buddhist class on a Thursday night. Daniella happened to live around the corner, and so did her friend Carla, with her boyfriend Daniel. One night, I introduced Daniella to a handful of my friends, including Jules, Toni, Liz and Meg at a Vietnamese restaurant in Marrickville. White lace curtains surrounded the windows, and the tablecloths were pink; it was my favourite. Jules had a few wines under her belt and turned to Daniella and said, "You can't speak English, and you don't even know how to use chopsticks."

She belly laughed at her own obnoxious comment. I felt Daniella's energy flatten, and on the drive home, she said, "I don't think your friend Jules likes me?"

"Don't worry about her," I replied. "She is just teasing. When people take the piss out of you here, it generally means they like you."

"Take a piece?" she responded. I giggled at her comment and didn't correct her.

"It's just a term, and Jules gets like that when she has a few drinks." From that night on, Daniella was nicknamed 'Brazil'.

Daniella was a hard worker; she got up at 4am to catch public transport across the Sydney Harbour Bridge to make sandwiches, pastries and quiches. She would often work nights or weekends at events to earn extra money. Dad's mum, Nan, died, and I was given some money to buy a one-bedroom unit in Coogee, my first home.

Six months into our relationship, Daniella moved in. My unit was situated at the top of two sets of stairs, an art deco block of four. The ceilings were ornate, and the bedroom looked out towards Coogee Beach, and I could see glimpses of the water. One bedroom, one bathroom, a sunroom and shared laundry. I loved this little place of safety and peace.

Daniella was my first real long-term relationship, that being anything over three years. She was born and raised in São Paulo, Brazil. She became a part of my family, and I was committed. We also flew to Brazil, where I met her family, and stayed in her parents' home. I couldn't understand what they were saying, and they could not understand me. Despite language barriers, our communication persisted, often involving light-hearted comments, predominantly directed at Daniella.

By that stage in our relationship, we were known as the Lindas. In Portuguese, Linda means gorgeous, so that's what we affectionately called each other. We were in love, and we shared some amazing times together, ignoring any red flags like the first gut feeling. Energetically, I sensed anger.

Daniella was a perfect match in many ways, as our dynamic developed, so did the cracks, of which we both played our part. Our first trip away was with Jules and her partner, Sarah. We went up to Queensland for the weekend and hired a house. On the second day, we went out white water rafting, and as we headed into the lobby to collect our group photos, a woman walked towards me, and we caught eye contact, nothing sexual, just eye contact. Daniella lost it.

"That woman just looked at you!" she said in a heightened voice. We were all new to Daniella's behaviour and made jokes to try and soothe her anger.

"Maybe she wants Shelley?" said Jules, sniggering.

"Do you want to fuck her, Shelley? You do, don't you?!" Daniella screamed.

"What? I...."

Before I could finish my sentence, Daniella stormed off in a tantrum. I was left bewildered, and Sarah followed Daniella to console her.

"What the fuck just happened?" I said to Jules.

"I like Brazil, but geez, she's a fiery one, Shell, good luck," she replied.

Daniella's vivacious and highly protective demeanour enabled me to hide. I was able to hide in my insecurity. I started hiding so much, I lost myself. I stopped putting myself first, and all the little, tiny cups full of faith and hope that I'd filled during my Buddhism practice got packed away. Daniella grew into a confident woman; her English excelled. She was one of those people so determined that when they did something, it was always done with excellence. My role as a caretaker was highlighted; not only did I have Mum and Gran, but now I had Daniella.

Daniella liked someone to look after her, the way a mother might look after a child. I took control of our life, as that is what I knew best.

"I've got this," became my modus operandi. I made all

the big decisions in the relationship, packed lunches and was the provider. That was my thing. I just did it. I shut down emotionally, and we became two lost and lonely people trying to navigate our trauma from the past with no real tools to do so.

As the cracks widened in our relationship, so did the intensity of our arguments. Our neighbours to the right, aka 'The Battlers', were a young couple with a baby. Blake, Lisa and Shayna. Blake was a good-looking man with a lean, muscular body. He was a little shy at times and worked as a labourer. Lisa was thin, tiny, friendly and worked in a bank. Shayna was invisible; we never heard a peep.

Blake's parents had bought the one-bedroom unit for him, and as Shayna grew older, she would sleep on the floor. The police were very familiar with the Battlers at Mount Street. Most weekends, Blake would come home blind drunk, fall into the bushes and then the verbal and physical abuse would start.

The sound of screaming voices and thudding noises echoed through the concrete walls, where Blake had given Lisa a black eye or fallen into the wall. I always worried about Shayna in all of it. Daniella and I lived next door to them for five years. Lisa's mum was a rough piece of work and would stand outside our front door smoking, leaving cigarette butts in my runners. I decided to confront her one day and ask for this not to happen again.

"Aww, ya fuckin, homo," she replied. I never left my shoes at the front door after that day. I always called the cops. I had seen enough of the end result of domestic violence during my thirteen years of policing, and I felt I had a duty of care. Daniella didn't share the same feelings; she was perhaps scared of them, and I guess coming from Brazil, she had seen what people could do in retaliation.

On one occasion, I grabbed my phone, and Daniella reached out to stop me.

"Don't call the cops!" she yelled.

"There is a child in there," I whispered as loud as I could.

"I don't care!" she said.

"Well, I do! Now let me go," I said as I pushed her away from me.

I felt suffocated; this was not the first time that Daniella would not allow me to have space or to pin her fears on me, so I felt even more determined to get out of that unit. I managed to get out of the door, and she was right behind me.

"Shell, Shell, Linda! Wait!" she screamed, her voice panicked.

I quickly jumped in Peggy, started the engine. Thud! Daniella threw herself onto my bonnet.

"Please don't leave!" she said, her voice now desperate. I turned the engine off. I could feel my chest getting hot, my cheeks flushed.

"Fucking just let me have some fucking space!" I yelled.

Daniella slid off the bonnet.

"You can't do that, you can't just leave, that's not fair," she said. I sensed her anger had not dissipated. People in the street were looking.

"I just need ten minutes to calm down," I retorted. My anger had not left me either.

I walked away, and Daniella placed her hand on my arm.

"Just leave me the fuck alone," I cried.

'You don't understand, where I come from, you would never open the door if neighbours were fighting, or call the police.'

It was becoming clear that we came from different worlds. One of the reasons Daniella left Brazil was that she was kissing a woman in a car late at night, and two guys surrounded them. They made them get out of the vehicle, and one of them placed a gun to Daniella's head. I strongly believe that moment traumatised her. The entire experience just reminded me of a quote I'd seen somewhere but wasn't sure who'd said it: "The universe is not short on wake-up calls; we are just too quick to hit the snooze button."

By this stage, I decided that I would embark on a Degree in Psychotherapy. My interest in the human psyche, attachment styles and mental health always intrigued me. I left labouring and worked part-time in the fitness industry.

***

By 2013, the Battlers had both lost their jobs, Shayna had been removed from her parents, and they were desperately selling the street drug 'Ice' from their unit. Eventually, they had to sell their home. It was a sad ending for them and a sigh of relief for us, their neighbours. Prior to this, Daniella and I had bought a Burmese kitten called Sunnie. Sunnie was my rock. I began focusing my attention on the cat, as I felt we had a special connection. Daniella preferred dogs but was fond of all animals, including Sunnie.

After completing my degree in Psychotherapy, my mother's health declined with frequent falls leading to hospital visits. I transported her back and forth, and she eventually received a metal plate in her elbow. Daniella was getting as much ink on her body as she could. The tattoos suited her. Her whole looked changed. Her long hair was gone and replaced with short, spunky haircuts. Every month, it was something new.

"How is my hair?" she asked repeatedly. She became fixated on her look.

We started attending regular gay dance parties, called 'I Remember House'. The music was right up my alley.

We both couldn't get enough and danced with our hands in the air to funky deep house music. It became the thing we did together, and we looked like the happiest couple on the dancefloor. Daniella was always kissing me and grabbing me, and watching to see who was looking at her. She had many women and men looking at her.

She looked like a Brazilian version of the singer Pink; chunky muscles, heaps of tats, sexy, a great dancer and cheeky. Her androgynous look was adored and swooned over. I was proud that 'Linda' was my partner; she exuded fun and warmth.

We enjoyed training together and often competed in gym sessions or runs. However, I craved deeper communication and vulnerability, which we couldn't achieve as a couple. This left me feeling unheard and shut down. There were many great things about the Lindas. My family embraced her, and she embraced them as her own. Often, I would remind myself of the best parts, but I knew deep down we weren't the best versions of ourselves in this relationship.

Daniella and I would often walk to Coogee Beach for a swim. It wasn't uncommon for Daniella to try and hold my hand, yet I felt uncomfortable being gay in my neighbourhood.

"Come on, Linda, let's walk down Coogee Bay Road," she said, grabbing my hand. I tried to pull away, and

Daniella squeezed my hand tighter and tried to kiss me.

"Please, not with all these people around staring at us, I feel uncomfortable," I said.

Daniella would not let go until I managed to wriggle out of her grip. Daniella laughed.

"Oh, Linda," she said, trying to kiss me again. After trying tirelessly to be heard, I focused on caregiving and neglected my own needs instead. The tantrums and mood swings happened regularly and became the norm. I felt depleted and in an endless battle of soothe, recover, rescue, repeat. I was scared to leave and just as afraid to stay.

Constant text messages and the need for reassurance became overwhelming. Initially, I enjoyed her affection, but we both changed over the years. Despite using various tactics—staying calm, seeking therapy, setting boundaries—I grew exhausted. I even consulted a sex therapist, wrongly blaming myself for our lack of intimacy.

My therapist highlighted the obvious.

"When you don't feel safe, how can you be vulnerable and allow your partner to touch you, which is an intimate and vulnerable exchange?" she told me.

The next few days, I tried out my homework, which was to begin setting boundaries.

"When I feel you disengage from our conversation, I feel unheard," I said, trying to apply the language the therapist had recommended.

This didn't last long. We were not aligned and ended up enraged. I likely suffocated her with control and caretaking. Eventually, we found safety in dysfunction, and both of us continued to project our trauma onto each other.

As the years progressed, nothing seemed to change. The anger, reactivity, blame and walking on eggshells continued. I was almost at breaking point, and we were arguing a lot. I felt lost and alone, and constantly tried to soothe Daniella's anxiety or tantrums.

Maybe if we move out of the small one-bedroom apartment in Coogee, she can have her dog, and things will be different? I'm an over-functioner, and perhaps my secondary gain in this relationship is to feel useful; after all, I helped her become a Citizen of Australia and supported her as my de facto in the immigration process. If I were to end this relationship, how would I feel? That I've failed, and it would reinforce my shame? I am useless, I'm a mistake, I am not capable of a relationship.

I wrote in my journal:

"The truth is, your relationship is in trouble because you set it up that way. If you are living a dysfunctional relationship with another person, it's because you have a dysfunctional relationship with yourself". UNKNOWN

One Friday night, I suggested that we go out for dinner somewhere different.

"Come on, let's go out for dinner?" I asked.

"Where?" Daniella said abruptly.

"Let's try somewhere new, like the Lebanese place?" I suggested.

Daniella immediately responded. "No, I don't like Lebanese food."

"What about the Japanese?" she said

"We always go there, but sure, let's go to the usual. Shall we grab a wine from the bottle shop around the corner?" I said, feeling disappointed.

"You mean the one where that homeless man sits out front begging for money? I don't like him," she said.

I felt on edge like she wanted an argument.

"He is harmless, and you just never know people's stories," I replied in defence of the homeless man.

"Why doesn't he just live in a fucking shelter, rather than begging everyone for alcohol?" Daniella scoffed. Her tone was aggressive, and my diplomatic approach fell on deaf ears.

We grabbed a bottle of wine, and I thought I would ask the guy in the bottle shop about the homeless man.

"Just a question, what's the story with the guy out on the street?"

"Oh, you mean David? He has a fear of the indoors, and the community offered to pay his rent. He doesn't drink, he bums a few ciggies though," he replied.

Daniella's judgment had come from seeing people live in the favelas of Brazil. Some people had jobs, and it was a functioning community.

Or maybe it was a projection; like you are Aussie, you have opportunities here, you have welfare, not like Brazil.

I told her what the bottle shop man said. Her energy softened as we walked in silence to the regular sushi train.

15

At Peace

Mum's depression gathered more momentum, so did her bouts of mini strokes, falls, lack of nourishment and increased addiction to valium and alcohol. She tried so hard to put on a brave face, to grin and bear it, to say to the world, 'I'm okay', yet her mind and physical body were suffering.

The fact that her mother of 98 years old was healthier and looked after Mum was a good reason to keep on pushing through. Each week at the RSL, it was a battle to get them both in and out of the car; Mum with a walking stick, and Gran with her wheelie walker. Mum's drop-down menu of conditions left her riddled in pain:

heart disease, emphysema, strokes, depression, anxiety, osteoporosis and anorexia.

Her spine was so sore she now sat sleeping in a chair all night. She did not have a bed in her one-bedroom unit. Her unit was tidy and well organised and decorated nicely. An electric IBM typewriter with pages of notes in shorthand surrounded the desk that occupied the space where a single bed would have been. The smell of cigarettes lingered on the walls as she blew smoke out of the kitchen window.

It was 7pm on a Monday night when Gran called. This was the same time that Mum and Gran usually shared a wine and a meal together. Gran did all the cooking, a salmon mornay or asparagus mornay, and rice was normally the favourite.

"Your mother doesn't look well, she looks dishevelled, and she seems a bit delirious; she wasn't making a lot of sense tonight," Gran said in a monotone voice over the phone.

"Ok, Gran, I'll give her a call," I said.

"Hey Mum, it's me, are you ok?" I rang.

"I'm not feeling the best. I think I just need to sleep. My elbow is swollen and hot; let's talk in the morning. I just need to rest," she said.

"Ok, just call me if you need me," I said. The phone went dead, and the clink of the receiver echoed in my ear.

The next morning, Gran called.

"Joy has been taken by ambulance to Manly Hospital," she said.

"Ok, I'll get there."

Fuck, fuck, fuck, my car has been broken down for a few days, and I'm across the other side of the Sydney Harbour Bridge. Why didn't I call an ambulance last night? How am I going to get there quickly?

I couldn't ask Daniella as she was at work, so I called Dad.

"Hey Matey," he said as he answered my call.

"Dad… would it be ok if I borrowed your car? Mum is in the hospital and my car is broken down," I said.

"What the fuck is wrong with your car?" he said.

"I think it's the engine," I replied.

"For fucks sake, your mother! Ok, come and get it, I will need it back by this arvo though!" he said.

"Yes, of course. I'll walk up to your place now," I said.

I hung up and briskly walked for fifteen minutes to get to Dad's. I could not think straight. As soon as I arrived, I jumped in the car and drove quickly to the hospital. I arrived in forty-five minutes to Gran, waiting in the old, rundown Manly Hospital.

Mum looked terrible—her skin was pale and sweaty, her head drooping, and she seemed vulnerable. Her elbow was red and hot.

"Your mum is septic, and we need to wash her elbow out and get rid of the bacteria, but we aren't equipped to do that here, so we have to transfer her to Royal North Shore Hospital," the doctor said.

I joined Mum in the brokenness of our reality. Another hospital visit. I was resentful and depleted. It felt like my twenties and thirties were consumed with a pattern of Mum getting sick, Mum having a fall, and Shelley being there.

Where is her brother Allan? He lives 10 minutes from Mum, how selfish of me to have these thoughts…

I waited for four hours, constantly checking the time.

"Mum, I have to get Dad's car back, so I will see you at Royal North Shore Hospital first thing in the morning."

"I will be ok, you go," Mum replied.

I got back to Dad's house around 3pm. Dad had been at the Bondi Junction RSL club all morning and had already had about six schooners. Visions of Mum flashed through my mind, like the dead bodies in the police station. Once you'd seen it, you couldn't unsee it.

"How is your mother, wanna beer?" he slurred.

"She has a septic elbow; she looks like shit. Thanks for the offer, but it has been a big day, and I just want to get home."

"Well, best you keep the car for a bit. We can use Alice's car."

"Oh, really? Thanks, Dad. I will get mine fixed as soon as I can," I promised.

Daniella got home around 6pm with a pizza from work, and I told her about my day as Sunnie snuggled between us on the couch.

"Oh, Linda, I'm so sorry about your mum," she said, wrapping her arms around me. I felt comforted and vulnerable as I cried on her shoulder. The next morning, I headed off early to avoid peak-hour traffic. Daniella was working a double lunch and dinner shift at a busy Italian restaurant in Alexandria.

I arrived at RNSH at 7.30am, familiar with every corner. In the six-bed ward, Mum had just had her elbow surgery. She sat in bed, tearful and miserable, her hair limp and stuck to her head. It was just Mum and me. Her voice was small as she spoke.

"It's nice to see you," she said.

"You too, Mum."

I sat gently at the end of her bed and touched her hand.

"It will be ok, you can get through this. I'm here, and Gran is on her way," I said, assuringly.

"I feel like such a burden," she said.

I gingerly swept the strands of thin hair from her face with no words. I was not used to touching Mum. I held back my tears.

This woman, my mother, has been through so much. I have nothing but compassion right now.

"Can you bring me my cigs next time?"

"Maybe, but I don't think it is a good idea to smoke after all this Mum," I said.

"Fine, but how would you feel being stuck in here? It's not too much to ask," Mum said defiantly.

Upon arriving home, I drank myself to sleep on the couch next to Sunnie. I missed my mother dearly; reminiscing about the way she used to be was challenging and evoked deep sadness. The sound of Daniella's scooter woke me. Having not eaten all day, I appreciated the slightly warm pizza. Daniella entered, embraced me, and I began to cry. Deep, guttural sobs.

A week later, I secured a new position as a counsellor on the Beyond Blue telephone helpline for anxiety and depression. The training centre was conveniently located near RNSH, allowing me to visit my mum during lunch breaks. I would drive to pick Gran up from Manly, return to North Sydney, then back to Manly, and finally home to Coogee. Unfortunately, few people visited Mum. Allan and his wife came occasionally, but my grandmother was unable to afford taxis and found it difficult to use public transport due to her age. Daniella would visit as often as she could.

I started to Google Sepsis, and this is what I read. "A potentially life-threatening condition that arises when the body's response to infection causes injury to its own tissues and organs[1]". Her elbow was still infected, and other little wounds started to appear. At 9pm, two weeks into my new job, I received a phone call from the hospital. It was a nurse.

"Your mother has gone into the ICU," she explained.

A short time later, I found myself sitting by mum's side, in the large single-bed ICU room. She was in an induced coma and couldn't breathe without a machine. Her mouth imposed with a plastic tube, and her veins were jabbed with a cannula to give her fluids.

This is enough of the pain and suffering.

"Mum, go and see all the kittens, I think you will be happy there," I said. Mum loved cats. The nurse, doctor and I stood around my mum, Joy, just the three of us. The doctor turned to me and asked if I wanted to call someone.

"Your mum won't last long once we take the tubes out; maybe twenty-four hours," he said.

---

[1] Katugume, B., Muzungu, J., Okello, N., & Namutebi, D. (2025). *Prevalence of neonatal sepsis and associated factors among neonates admitted in the neonatal intensive care unit at Lira Regional Referral Hospital, Northern Uganda.* PLoS One, 20(1), e0315794.

I went outside into the cold corridor and called Daniella.

"Hey, it's me. The doctors reckon Mum has twenty-four hours to live."

'Ok, I'll come over," she said.

I met Daniella in the main foyer of the hospital. She hugged me tight. Words were unspoken as the hug lingered.

"The doctor wants to take the tubes out, and he thinks it will be quick," I said.

Daniella looked puzzled.

"What do you mean? She isn't dead?" she asked.

'Well, no, not yet," I replied.

"Oh fuck, I just told work that she was dead. That's why I had to leave," she said, clearly agitated.

"What am I going to say to work now?" she continued, her voice panicked.

"Just tell them the truth. They are not going to fire you because you made a mistake," I said calmly.

'Fuck, I'm going to have to say she is dead. I will look like an idiota!" she cried.

"Just go back to work, I can manage this," I said, sensing her discomfort.

"No, I'm here now," Daniella said. We took the lift to Level 6: Intensive Care Unit, Room 2. Daniella burst into tears. I put my hand on her back and held it there for a moment. A few minutes later, the doctor walked in with the nurse. The four of us stood over Mum.

"Ok, we are going to take the tubes out, the ones that assist her staying alive, and given your mother's weight, she will probably go quickly," the doctor said.

The airway tubes were gently removed, and we waited for the expected last breath.

***

Hours went by, and the doctor and the nurse had long left the room. I leaned into Mum's ear.

"I give you permission to let go, Mum. Remember all the good times we had in the Blue Mountains," I whispered.

Daniella placed her hand on my mother's forehead.

"It's ok, Joy. You can let go now," she said. It was getting dark, and Mum was still alive.

I visited daily. Dad came for a brief visit one day but left shortly afterwards; he just couldn't face it. Mum was later moved to a single room in the ward for palliative care. The room was dimly lit, and the sounds of nurses' voices outside provided some relief to the death rattle – Mum's laboured and gurgled breathing. She was a fighter, and both the hospital staff and I were amazed that she was still alive.

What is she waiting for?

A few months prior, Daniella and I had booked flights to Byron Bay for a friend's fiftieth birthday. Mum was a private person, self-conscious until the day she died. My intuition told me to go to Byron Bay. I followed my gut after seven long days of what should have been a quick passing. The family all said goodbye.

Besides, other people can visit, right?

May 11, 2013, just happened to be Mother's Day. Mum was 62 years old. Daniella hired a car from Ballina Airport, and as we drove down the treelined, red dirt driveway into the sound of voices roaring, my phone rang. It was 6pm.

"Your mother has passed," the doctor said on the other end of the line.

I wasn't surprised; it was as if she waited, knowing I would be with friends. I was not in the mood for a party, yet I pushed through, seeing that Daniella appeared to be having fun. The dawn broke, and Daniella and Meg were drinking a beer.

"I think I need to go home," I said.

"Oh, really, just a little longer?" Daniella replied.

Meg quickly turned to Daniella.

"For fuck sake, Brazil, your girlfriend's mum just died," she snapped.

"It's ok, we are both just finding ways to cope" I said to Meg.

Upon returning to Sydney, I was responsible for organising the cremation, notifying the banks, and sorting through my mother's belongings, which was particularly challenging. While going through her folder by her IBM typewriter, I discovered a script she had written about a murder, with characters resembling family members and my mother as the lead role. I started reading:

"Adjusting to death, the sudden absence of a strong family member is extremely difficult. A strange, lost feeling can overtake. A quivering inside, afraid of choosing the correct future path, which will feel lonely.

Depression is a word - a curse indeed. Silent and deadly at its worst, thoughts naturally move to a final release from pain and heartache, irrespective of any cruel, sad repercussions. A bittersweet pill to swallow when there is no other way out. Chronic pain is so debilitating and continual, always lurking in the background, to creep in and spoil the moment, slowly reducing one's stamina.

The body can only take so much before it must seek an escape from the continual burden, whilst the mind wanders dangerously to all areas seeking solace, no matter the consequences. Would such a selfish act cause too much heartache for others to endure who don't deserve it? Eventually, time would hopefully heal the wound, although its remaining scar would always inhibit the bearer from moving on, perhaps quietly attempting to handle life as it now presents. It is wise to remember that the sufferer must often put on a brave face where appropriate, to meet society's demands in the company of friends and loved ones.

A heavy burden indeed. Those never experiencing such would not fully understand its dimensions."

My heart sank.

Mum really just wanted to die.

I sat alone amongst the pages of regret and sadness with a deep sense of compassion as I let the tears merge into her private world.

16

Byron Bay

One year after Mum died, Gran was living in a nursing home. At age 99, she had all her marbles, yet she struggled with reflux and hated living in the nursing home environment, where others could not talk and needed to be fed. Gran would spend most days in her room, unless her son Allan or I would take her to the RSL for a seniors' meal. Daniella had Mondays off, and we went to visit Gran. Daniella and Gran were close. We walked into her single bedroom. Gran was dressed in a white blouse and her favourite brown winter coat. Gran's hair had just been permed, and she even wore her white stoned brooch pinned to the corner of her coat. My grandmother's pants were neat, and her shoes were in impeccable condition; she looked ready for lunch.

"Hey, Gran," I said.

"Hey, Helen," Daniella said as we poked our heads into her room. After some small talk, Gran said, "I have something I want to tell you girls."

It sounded serious.

"Ok, Gran," I said with uncertainty.

Gran was sitting on her bed, shoes and all.

"I have decided I'm not going to eat anymore. It's time," she said.

Daniella and I started crying

'There is no need for tears," she said in a matter-of-fact tone.

"What about the letter from the Queen? You turn 100 next month?" I replied

"Oh, I don't need all that fuss," she said.

A week later, on the 11th of August 2014, Gran passed away.

I suggested to Daniella that we move to Byron Bay. I had no more commitments in Sydney, and my new job allowed me to work anywhere in Australia. Daniella was hesitant, plus she loved her job waitressing. I thought it would give us a fresh start. There are many myths and stories about Byron Bay. Someone once told me that people come to heal, and if you don't, the energy of the land will spit you out.

We packed up the car at approximately 5am in May 2015, with Sunnie in her crate. As usual, an argument ensued, given our apprehension about the impending change. Three weeks earlier, we had flown to Byron and secured a suitable home by signing a lease agreement within one hour of our flight home.

It must be a sign; this is going to work.

Upon arrival, we felt a heightened sense of excitement as we moved into a single-story, three-bedroom house with a backyard, located near the beach. Neither of us had any support or friends in the area.

The next day, we walked down the main street, encountering tourists, hippies, and the homeless—each contributing to Byron's uniqueness. The energy felt special with the ocean's roar and birds' whistles on Bundjalung land, believed to have healing powers. Though cliché, I welcomed the lifestyle change.

"I can't believe you made me come here, this place is disgusting, dirty, with smelly hippies everywhere!" Daniella turned to me.

"This is only one part of Byron that you are seeing; there is much more," I said with conviction.

We always travelled to Byron on holidays, so some of it was familiar, and as tourists, Daniella and I both loved it, a small a quirky town surrounded by incredible beaches. In the beginning, friends would come and visit. That part was fun. Sunnie was adjusting to the new environment at six years old.

Daniella transitioned from hospitality to a job at St George Bank due to her excellent customer service skills. She met the CEO while serving him in Sydney, learned about the new branch in Byron, interviewed and got hired.

Moving from waitressing to banking set her on a new career path. Daniella initially disliked Byron and felt unqualified to work in a bank. She struggled with her new job at first, often coming home in tears.

I also felt the pressure at work when I was trained up for a Domestic Violence Hotline, 1800 Respect. I was five years into my role, and on many occasions, I had people calling wanting to commit suicide, abusing me, and the regulars that wanted attention, or were just lonely. Between depression and anxiety calls, and now domestic violence, the vicarious trauma was starting to take its toll.

I started journaling in between calls. I knew Daniella and I were in a tumultuous relationship, I didn't want my relationship to fall apart, I didn't want to acknowledge my reality, and deep down I knew that I was attached to the 'what was', and clinging to 'what if'. My avoidant side completely shut down, as each caller represented a part of us that kept us together, and that part was trauma. We functioned in a trauma bond, rescuing, enabling, chronic fears of abandonment, and were emotionally addicted to each other. My protection from this truth was to emotionally abandon Daniella, even further. Things did not improve, Sunnie died, and we both felt alone and isolated in our demise.

I started researching rescue dogs in between calls. I found Lola, a mixed-breed, medium-sized kelpie cross. Her brown eyes were incredibly soulful, almond-shaped, and her gaze soft, unbroken. I could not stop looking at her photo, plus I knew Daniella would love a dog. In my five-minute break one night, I called Daniella into my office to show her Lola.

"Look, look at her eyes, what do you think?" I said.

"Yeah, maybe, are you sure we are ready for a dog?" Daniella replied.

"Maybe I can go and see her, they say dogs choose their owners, don't they?"

Daniella walked off and grabbed a beer, and rolled a ciggie.

This could be a new beginning for us.

My enquiry about Lola was unsuccessful; she had been taken, but Melissa, her sister, was available. Melissa didn't have Lola's eyes. A few days later, the rescue place called to say Lola was available again because the previous customer disliked the grey bits on her nose. Daniella had come around to the idea of Lola, and some excitement stirred between us.

Another sign.

On my day off, I drove to Queensland to meet Lola; she ran to the front door, literally smiling. I just knew she was meant to be a part of our lives; her legs were very long for a 3-month-old medium-sized dog, but I didn't care. What do I know about dogs, except that we both connected and that meant everything. I drove straight to St George Bank with Lola to show Daniella. I texted her first.

"Come out the front and meet Lola."

Daniella smiled from ear to ear and kissed Lola's head multiple times through the car window. We found a new distraction, a new love, a new way to communicate, a communication based on Lola. We took her for walks on the beach, we met people, we met friends with other dogs, yet my feelings of loneliness and depression remained.

Lola was a happy, friendly giant by the time she grew into her long legs, looking much like a greyhound cross than a kelpie or cattle dog. We all trusted each other. It was not long before our relationship turned in the usual direction. Rinse and repeat. Slamming doors and sleeping on the edge of the bed was the norm. Lola became frightened when we argued, and to this day still cowers if a door is to blow shut. Through all the ups and downs, we kept hanging on and even bought a house together in Queensland. On the day of settlement, we decided to have a beer at the Beach Hotel in Byron.

"Cheers, Linda, I love you," I said.

"Cheers, Linda, I love you too," Daniella replied as we walked away from the bar looking for a spot to sit. It was crowded and we had to share a table, that's where we met Bella. Bella was vivacious and chatty and lived in the area.

"Hey girls, I'm Bella, you look like you are celebrating?"

"Yeah, we just bought a house in Queensland" I said.

"Congrats, girls," Bella said as she clinked our beer glasses.

Bella was from the country, so there was a lot of Australian slang. She had an infectious nature, wearing an old man's checkered style beret, a flannel shirt, jeans and RM William boots.

"So do you chicks live here or are you a pair of Queenslanders?"

"No, we live here in Byron," Daniella was quick to correct her.

"Ok, cool, then you must meet my peeps in Feddy, maybe you can come over one day and I can play you some tunes," Bella said.

"I would love that," I said with excitement.

Yay, a friend!

My first visit to Feddy/Federal was alone. Bella lived underneath a gay couple, Sam and Tarni and their son David. I drove through the hills of Byron and arrived at the church. It literally was a church with exquisite leadlight windows, Cathedral ceilings, arched doorways, and a beautiful outlook through the enormous native trees, towards mountain ranges. Bella played some tunes as we sat outside, surrounded by three Kelpies, Atlas Bellas's dog and Blossy and Bella, who belonged to the girls upstairs.

"Wanna dart and a vino Shell?"

"Sure" I said as Bella rolled me a ciggie and handed me a chilled glass of Pinot Gris. Daniella was at work, and Bells and I sat and chatted for hours. I felt comfortable around Bells, and we became good friends. Around 3pm, Sam got home from work. Sam was like Daniella, masculine and muscular, and loved a chat. I arrived home that afternoon, excited to tell Daniella about my day with Bells.

"I had such a great day today, Linda! I met Atlas, Bella's dog and Sam, one of the girls who lives upstairs. Bella played music, and you have to see Federal, it's stunning!" I gushed.

"Good for you. I am not sure about Bella; she seems a bit cocky."

"Oh," I said, feeling a little deflated. "Sam and Bells invited us for lunch on the weekend 'cause they want us to meet Tarni too, she is off work this weekend, she is a nurse."

"I'll see, probably not my thing, and I am tired from work," Daniella replied.

As it turned out, Daniella and I ended up at the

church on the weekend. Tarni was a great cook, and David and Daniella would practice their push-ups whilst Tarni cooked her special Middle Eastern lamb. Bells complemented the dish with a smashing salad. Sam and I drank and chatted, Sam mostly commenting on how fit David and Daniella were.

Sam also liked to keep busy, showing me around.

"Come and look at the bathroom, this is where the priest used to get dressed, oh, and you have to come and check out the citrus in the yard, and I love native plants like the Elaeocarpus Eumindi."

Sam went on to explain about Australian Native plants, and her passion was exuberant. We headed back to the others, and Daniella had relaxed and was her charming self.

17

A Mess

Tarni had the prettiest blue eyes I had ever seen. She was feminine, voluptuous with large, round hips and breasts; she exuded sexuality. I hadn't really seen a bigger girl who was confident with their body. We all became a tribe, an inseparable pack.

As the friendship developed, Tarni and I became close, and we found ourselves having deep conversations. We both had been with our partners for nine years, and an emotional affair began; we could not wait to catch up. Our connection was extremely rich, and Tarni became incredibly attractive. I didn't think it was possible that I could be attracted to someone outside of the average Body Mass Index scale; my mother would freak out, and I had forgotten my Buddhist lesson, "cherish all living beings". I was in judgment and ego, and as soon as I recognised this, my biggest lesson came toward me like a gust of wind so sudden it uprooted my legs and threw me on the ground.

Daniella, Toni, plus some others had settled in on a picnic rug with drinks and snacks at a festival in Bangalow, chatting and watching people go by. I decided to head up to the Bangalow pub and have a beer with Tarni and Sam, leaving Daniella with our friends. When I came back, the girls were packing up, and Daniella's body language was angry, face frowning, arms flapping. I was in trouble. Daniella was not shy to show her feelings in public.

"What took you so long?" she yelled.

Our friends walked ahead. I stopped and sat on a tree stump with my head down in silence as Daniella was reprimanding me like a child. She was not shy to express her feelings in public, and I could not look up at the people entering the festival. I felt humiliated and broken. That was my tipping point. Daniella and I went home. A few days later, I looked at her, scared of her reaction to what I was about to say.

"I can't be in this relationship anymore, I have feelings for Tarni," I said.

"What! You are leaving me for that fat bitch," she yelled.

I know I have deeply hurt Daniella, and I did my usual

trick, find someone else, run, except this felt different.

Daniella and I continued living together, sleeping in separate rooms. Tarni left Sam and moved in with her mother. It was a mess.

* * *

Three months later, I was rostered on the usual Sunday 7am shift, counselling callers via 1800 Respect and Beyond Blue. The calls were coming in at a velocity I found hard to handle. I would switch my introduction methodically between domestic violence callers and depression and anxiety. The nature of the calls would often co-exist, and I was used to that, yet something inside me had reached breaking point, and given my relationship was under strain, I was feeling less capable of dealing with others' trauma. I began to have flashbacks of my childhood, the police, and scenarios with Daniella. I felt like I needed to be on my own and run from the attraction towards Tarni and run from Daniella.

Was that not what I've always done? Run, just run…

I started researching volunteer programs in Southeast Asia, mainly to do with animals, rather than humans. It had to be a 'friendly' budget, and in between my trauma calls, I found the right place. I booked in February 2018.

My first stop was a well-frequented area by tourists, and then I was set to volunteer with elephants. I was to stay five days in a hut on my own. Volunteers were not allowed to touch the elephants. I liked that, as all the elephants had been abused or exploited in their time.

I thoroughly researched the project, finding that sunscreen, mosquito repellent, and appropriate clothing for jungle trekking were necessary. The website advised covering up during dusk and dawn in a malaria zone with long sleeves and pants or using mosquito repellent. The next day, I bought Bushman's Repellent spray and purchased travel pants, a long-sleeved top, and a hoodie from a Kathmandu store and prepared for my trip.

18

Mr Lim

FEBRUARY 3, 2018, I prepared for travel, saying goodbye to Daniella and Tarni, with an inner knowing that I needed clarity. I had seen a travel agent and booked a tidy hotel room in a decent part of Phnom Penh, Cambodia. It was my first solo journey overseas. I arrived in the morning in the hustle and bustle of Cambodia, with eyes wide open to the steady flow of people and traffic. I jumped in the nearest taxi and headed to my hotel. It was 11am, and the staff were eager to greet me.

"Sorry, ma'am, your room isn't ready, one hour?" the woman said, dressed in a traditional green silk wrap-around skirt featuring a delicate pattern, complemented by a lace white top and a matching silk sash draped over her shoulder. I left my bag and walked outside into the street. Vendors were hustling for me to buy cigarettes or soft drinks. I don't drink soft drinks, but I don't mind a cigarette every now and then, so I bought a packet. I walked further along the street to a large vacant area, surrounded by bench seats and temples in the background. As I sat down on the bench seat, there was no shade, and the air was hot. I was dressed in jeans and a long-sleeved shirt. Within a few minutes, I noticed a small, framed Cambodian man walking towards me; he had a towel around his neck, like he had just worked out. He stopped in front of me.

"Hi, I am Charlie," he said. His English was ok, with a few words missing from time to time.

"Where you come from?" he asked.

"I'm from Australia," I replied.

"How long you here for, what your plan?"

"I'm volunteering with elephants in the jungle, starting tomorrow."

"Oh, where about?" Charlie asked.

"I'm not sure how to say the name, but it is about eight hours from here, and then I am going to Siem Reap," I replied

Charlie nodded his head and pointed to the left.

"I work there at casino. I use to work at casino in Blacktown, Sydney."

"Oh, ok, I don't know many casinos in Blacktown," I said.

"You like gambling?" Charlie asked.

"I've only ever played Roulette."

"That rigged, they put magnets under da table, anyway you want to meet my sister Anna?" Charlie said enthusiastically. Since Charlie appeared friendly, I agreed while noting the time on my watch, expecting my room to be ready soon.

Anna was a short, unassuming Cambodian woman, possibly in her 60s, with a genuine smile and pleasant demeanour. After introductions, Anna inquired about my plans for the day, and I informed her I intended to visit the Russian markets. Anna offered to take me in a tuk-tuk. Her English was quite good, allowing us to communicate effectively. We agreed to meet at 1pm; it was now 12pm, giving me time to check in and shower. I appreciated the opportunity to be guided by a local, as navigating alone seemed daunting.

Anna was there waiting in her tuk-tuk at exactly 1pm; there was no sign of Charlie. I jumped in the back of the open-air cart, this time dressed for the weather in a pair of shorts and a t-shirt. Anna noticed my small over-the-shoulder bag.

"You make sure, you keep the bag at the front, and hold tight, bad people come and steal from you," she warned.

"Ok," I said as I twisted my bag to the front of my body and wrapped my arms around it.

"Have you eaten?' Anna asked.

"No," I said.

"Why don't you come to my house and I give you something to eat?"

That seems kind of her. I guess I should be open to new adventures away from the chaos at home.

"Sure," I replied.

I was feeling a sense of freedom and exhilaration, as we travelled along the dusty streets of Phnom Penh, horns honking, chaotic, intriguing, and I had no idea where I was. After what seemed like thirty minutes, we pulled up in a not-so-tidy area with small outdoor corridors that led us to a set of stairs.

"Come," Anna said. I walked into a weird kitchen, empty and stark, with a small bench against the wall. There was a young woman standing next to it. I was escorted upstairs to a clean room with a small dining table to my right. Upon a further scan, I noticed a shelf full of dolls, surrounded by white lace mats.

"This is Papa," Anna said. Papa was sitting on the couch to my left. He was a big man, with big hands, and a little tubby around his belly. I assumed he was Cambodian. Papa got up to greet me, while Anna poured us all a cup of tea. Papa's voice was loud and clear. His presence was slightly intimidating.

"I hear you like Roulette?" Papa asked.

'Well, I like it, but I rarely play," I responded, wondering what he was getting at.

"I used to work in a casino here; the roulette table was rigged, with magnets underneath."

"Oh, ok," I looked up at the doll's faces, all staring at me. My gaze was disrupted as Anna came up with lunch, a plate of Cambodian-style fish, and salad. The three of us moved to the dining table for lunch with a glass of water each. I was incredibly grateful for the hospitality; we made small talk, and after a very quick meal, Anna said, "Don't worry, we get to markets later."

Papa stood up from the table.

"Come on, I'll show you a great card game called Baccarat."

I had never heard of this game. Papa and Anna took me into another room. There was a double bed against the wall, with a table in front of it. A colourful quilt engulfed the bouncy mattress. Anna and I sat at the end of the bed, and Papa sat across from us in a plastic chair behind a wooden table. I was feeling unnerved, but nothing too major. I'd met nice people on holidays before. I sat with curiosity as Papa started shuffling the cards, so fast and so impressive, he had definitely worked in a Casino. His hand was quick as he placed a few cards face down. As he was about to turn the card, he said, "This will be Ace of Spades." Boom, just like that, the Ace of Spades was on her back.

"This is Queen of Diamonds." Flick, and turn, there she was; the Queen of Diamonds. This man seemed clever. The

Five of Clubs, the Three of Spades, and after six cards were turned, I was convinced this guy was a card shark.

Gran had taught me a few card games like Rummy and Gin Rummy. We played every chance we could; I enjoyed cards and was quick to learn the rules.

Baccarat is a card game played at casinos, often in rooms reserved for high-stakes players. It has a reputation for being associated with luxurious casinos around the world, including Monte Carlo and Las Vegas. While easy to play, experienced players often employ strategies to improve their chances of winning. Skill and luck both play a role in Baccarat. High-stakes players are known to watch for patterns in the game and use strategic methods by tracking probabilities, which can potentially increase their chances of winning. The game moves quickly, with the highest hand being Nine—Jacks, Queens, and Kings count as 0. Each hand starts with two cards, and a third may be dealt optionally. The hand closest to Nine wins.

"I'm going to show you some hand signals," Papa said. I was feeling a little nervous by now.

"If you put your index finger and thumb together, that means No, and if you cross your middle and index finger, that means Yes."

Papa showed me another hand signal, but I didn't understand it. He pushed a pile of colourful casino chips towards me. Moments later, a tall Chinese man in a yellow suit and bow tie walked in.

"This is Mr Lim, he will be playing with us today," said Papa. My heart started racing as Mr Lim popped open a silver briefcase to display a stash of American Dollars. It was like something out of Oceans Eleven. Everything was happening so quickly. A wad of cash was placed in a little silver tin next to Papa.

"Don't worry, I put $10,000 in for us," Papa said.

Mr Lim took a seat next to Papa. He was seated slightly back from Papa, not in alignment. Anna nodded at me with gentle encouragement. Papa was the banker and started shuffling and dealing the cards. Since Mr Lim could see the expressions on Papa's face, and I knew my Yes and No hand signals, we were seriously playing. Papa signalled to me with his eyes; I could tell if he wanted me to signal yes or no, and he dealt another card.

I was winning, and up to $25,000 US dollars. Anna was smoking a cigarette and offered me one. I took it, thinking it would help my nerves.

How did I get into this tiny bedroom? In the middle of Phnom Penh, with three strangers, suddenly playing a card game I had never heard of with a briefcase full of cash. Things could go terribly wrong; I have no idea where I am, and my mobile phone is on SOS.

Mr Lim looked unhappy, so Papa suggested pausing the

game for me to get some money. I was being asked many questions about my finances. Having recently sold a unit in Sydney, I had a good amount of money in the bank. We placed our cards and cash into labelled envelopes, "Shelley" and "Mr Lim", and put them in a silver tin. I went to grab my phone.

"Leave your phone, come," said Anna. I followed Anna back down towards the kitchen. Mr Lim stayed behind and waited in the room with the weird dolls and lace cloths. Next thing, I was whisked into a tuk-tuk. Their driver was waiting for us.

Anna started asking a lot of questions.

"Do you have husband?" said Anna.

"No," I said.

"Boyfriend?"

"No."

"We are going to be rich! Mr Lim is bad man, he illegally import cigarettes," Anna said.

"Where are we going?" I asked.

"To ATM," Anna replied.

"I haven't used an ATM in Cambodia. Does the cash come in Cambodian currency or American dollars?"

Anna got frustrated and spoke to the driver in Khmer. The driver pulled over, outside a large mall, and I was taken to a money exchange. By now, Anna's energy was rushed and frantic. She pointed at a thick gold necklace, and the shop assistant placed it on the counter. Anna and the shop assistant spoke in Khmer. Anna looked me dead in the eye; the unassuming woman had a vastly different approach now.

"$4000," she said without blinking an eye.

I feel like something sinister is going on, but I'm surrounded by Cambodian eyes everywhere.

I pulled my credit card out, bought the $4000 necklace, and we walked briskly back to the tuk-tuk. I hadn't seen daylight since 1pm, and the colour of the day had changed; it was a little darker. It felt like about 4pm. I felt completely vulnerable, like I wanted to trust.

I'm just playing a card game, right?

We went back to Papa's house, and Mr Lim and I entered the small bedroom again. The gold necklace was placed in the silver tin. The game started again. We played game after game until I was up $75,000 US dollars.

How will I fit this in my suitcase?!

Then, just like that, the game turned. I was now supposed to do the other hand signal, the one I had forgotten. I felt like I'd fucked up. Mr Lim kept winning and sitting on $100,000. Papa looked distressed. Finally, he called it.

"No more games." Papa signalled for me to follow him, and we walked into the hallway. I noticed the brown carpet as I dropped my head in shame. Papa's voice was elevated, his hands raised in the air. He then placed them on his head and screamed, "My family! How could you do this to my family?" I stood in silence for a moment.

"I'm sorry, I'm sorry!" I said, panicking. Papa calmed down, regulating his emotions.

"Don't worry, we get money back, I can get from casino, they will lend to me, in meantime, go back to your hotel and I call you."

I walked with Anna to the tuk-tuk waiting outside. There was now a new driver. It was dark outside, and I still had seen nothing of Phnom Penh; no Russian Markets, no temples, just a small Cambodian bedroom, a shopping mall, and a gold necklace which had been left as security in Papa's little silver tin. Life had come to the streets, with vendors haggling with tourists. Anna introduced me to Cam, our new driver. The energy was tense.

"You get Cambodian phone so we can call you," she demanded.

Cam pulled over to a dodgy mobile phone tent, and I purchased an old model orange Nokia mobile phone for $10.00 with a Cambodian SIM card. We travelled a few minutes down the road to the place I met Anna seven hours ago.

"Papa will call at 8.30pm. He let you know if he get money and we can keep playing Mr Lim," Anna said.

Feeling depleted, I walked back to my hotel room and slumped on the bed. I decided to open a cold beer and wait until 8.30pm. At 6.42pm, the orange Nokia lit up with a text in very broken English, which read:

"THE MONEY THAT I BORROW TODAY SUPPOSEDLY TO BRING TO SIEM REAP UR MONEY MAYBE CANNOT RETURN AS IT ALREADY WITH MR LIM."

At 7.04pm:

"PLS WAIT TOMORROW I TRY MY BEST GOOD NIGHT."

Then three minutes later:

"PLS U MUST REST I KNOW UR TIRED I CALL YOU TOMORROW."

I couldn't make sense of who was texting me, so I waited. At exactly 8.30pm, my little orange Nokia started buzzing. Ring Ring!

"It's me, Papa, I can't get money, but don't worry, Mr Lim happy to meet in Siem Reap. I'll call you on this phone, after you finish volunteering with elephant," he said. His voice was calm as he quickly hung up.

I think I have been scammed, maybe? I'm not sure. Everything just feels so surreal, and I just want to go home. Home to Tarni.

At 9.30pm, Tarni sent me a message on WhatsApp.

"How were the markets?"

"I have an adventure to tell you."

I called her and relayed what happened over the last seven hours. Tarni abruptly interrupted me.

"Listen to me, this is the craziest thing I have ever

heard, you're so vulnerable, they were never taking you to the markets! These types of people with cash are corrupt! I am sick with worry, you must keep in touch!" she screamed. Tarni was one to get a little dramatic, so I just played it cool.

"I'll be ok, sorry to upset you," I replied. The distress and elevation in her voice went up a few more notches.

"This is dangerous shit, babe. I'll give you $4000 when I get paid, I promise. Please don't leave the hotel room. This is not street smart, Shelley. Fuck the money, I am frightened for you, I'm in so much shock. It's a dangerous place for vulnerable tourists!" she continued.

"I am stupid, I know," I said. We said goodbye and hung up, and I turned my light out, pulling the fresh covers over my body to get some rest before my next stop, the one I came here for – the elephants.

***

I woke up still reeling from what had happened the day before. It was 3.14 am in Cambodia, and 7.15am back home in Australia. I was wide awake, scared and feeling vulnerable and alone in a strange country. I woke to the memories of my father's words, *"You are a dreamer, not a doer, just shut your stupid little mouth."*

The words from Dad rang like sirens in my head, blue and red flashing lights of danger, like something bad was about to happen.

I just need to make my way to the bus stop and get out of here.

I had one last conversation with Tarni that morning, and her anxiety levels had dropped; the reality of yesterday kicked in. I checked out at 6am and asked the reception to order a taxi.

19

The Elephants

I got on that bus to the jungle and felt a wave of relief, away from the trouble that I had just experienced. It was a long, treacherous bus ride, along dirty, narrow roads, and as we travelled further, the landscape became sparse; more dirt, fewer people. We stopped for lunch in an open outdoor kitchen, where the traditional dish of Cambodia was being cooked, "Amok", which translates to a coconut fish curry, and reminded me of Anna's lunch. I wasn't game to eat anything.

Just another five hours.

My mind was racing, recalling the events from the day prior.

At 5pm and I arrived at Pal Peam Village. The village was quaint with a lot of little shops, and as I got off the bus, no one haggled with me. I walked across the road to the office.

I can't say I've always had a love for elephants, but I was desperate to escape my reality. Besides, I was fit and healthy and trained hard most days. My body did what I wanted it to. I jumped on the back of an open 4WD with five other volunteers from around the world and headed further out into the jungle. I didn't care about Mr Lim, and my life in Byron Bay, I felt free and excited, and within ten minutes, I was deep in the jungle with no mobile reception.

We entered a wooden house characterised by high timber ceilings and a thatched roof made of durable straw. The main living room featured two old, comfortable armchairs, red cushions scattered on the floor, and small bookshelves to the side. The room offered a view of a lush green jungle. We were then shown the kitchen, where each vegetarian dish would be prepared and served. A fridge was available for purchasing cold beers, water, and soft drinks. I rested on a hardwood seat in the outdoor, open-air room, which was cozy with large terracotta tiles, hammocks, and the occasional healthy-looking cat. I sat and listened to Gretta, whose role was to explain the itinerary for the next five days.

"Welcome, thank you to everyone who is volunteering

to help the elephants and the community that supports these beautiful creatures. We have a small family of four elephants here, and each day our guides will share their stories as part of the volunteer program. We give you the opportunity to participate in various projects, such as helping out in the village with minor labour, and you will also be taken to a nearby school, where we will collaboratively give it a fresh look, with a colourful coat of paint. I will let you all introduce yourselves, and then one of our staff will assist you to your rooms. I must reinforce to wear insect repellent, particularly at dawn and dusk," she explained.

Most of the staff who worked on the project were travellers, many from England.

One of them, Scott, was assigned to show me to my hut, where I would be staying. I followed him down the hill, lined with rough concrete slabs in the shape of stairs, which trailed off to the left, where I noticed a terracotta statue of three tiny elephants stacked on top of each other. A little wooden sign was glued or nailed into the top of the first elephant; it read 3 Ning nest.

I really am in the jungle!

As I looked to the left, I saw my thatched roof hut; it had a slim sheet of colourbond type material leaning up against it, all the way to the tip of the roof. I noticed a few dents, but I did not pay too much attention. The place was rustic and gorgeous, and I was just happy to be alone and excited for the next five days ahead.

"Dinner is in thirty minutes, oh and by the way, there is a small hole in the roof, it will be fixed tomorrow," Scott said.

"No worries," I replied.

Before entering my hut, I saw a thick forest and a banana palm at my back door. Sunlight pierced the dense vegetation like two rays, cutting the shape of the number 1 twice. Inside was a simple double bed with a mosquito net tied to each post and a red quilt cover adorned with gold elephants. The terracotta tiles matched the theme.

I headed to the bathroom to freshen up. The old, faded tiles were clean, and a blue bucket sat next to the toilet. A ginger and white cat tried to reach the water. Stepping outside, I absorbed the scene: the setting sun, the active wildlife. Returning inside, the ginger cat was gone. The bathroom instructions read:

This is a cold water shower only. Please flush the toilet with the bucket provided. Many thanks.

After a fresh cold shower, I walked up to dinner, a little nervous to mingle, and exhausted from the harrowing bus ride. The servery was set out in a buffet style, and I grabbed a plate to walk around. I was happy that the food was vegetarian; it felt somehow safer. I took my seat next to an

English couple.

'Hey, I'm Shelley," I said.

"Nice to meet you! I'm Grace, and this is my partner Julie," one of them said.

I felt relieved to have some gays in the village. We did the usual chit chat, 'Where are you from?' 'How long have you been travelling?'

It turned out that they had been travelling around Asia for months. We all grabbed a beer and chatted after dinner in the open lounge room. By then, it was almost dusk. Both Julie and Grace sprayed themselves with insect repellent. They were already wearing long-sleeved pants and shirts. They seemed diligent about malaria prevention.

'Are you guys taking anti-malaria pills?" I asked curiously.

"Grace had meningitis from a mosquito on our last trip and was really ill, so we don't take the risk. You will find that most people here do not take the tablets; we have been here for two days already, and I asked a few other volunteers about the malaria tablets," said Julie.

I walked back to my room, not giving the meningitis story much thought. I wasn't even sure what happened if you had the illness; I was mostly familiar with Ross River fever because it was common back home in the Northern Rivers.

The next day, after breakfast, I went to see Samba, an

elephant. Samba was brought to Southeast Asia after the civil war. She had become a permanent feature, giving rides to tourists. After thirty years in the city, her owner decided to retire her to this land. Samba met Suby here and learned how to socialise and live in the forest. I had not been particularly curious about elephants before; I mainly came to observe and experience life in a different way, yet I soon discovered how an elephant can capture the heart.

Samba was 57 years old and weighed 3.2 tonnes! Each day, her feet would be soaked in iodine. They were sore and damaged from plodding the steaming pavement of Phnom Penh, carrying the weight of the unaware traveller. Her feet had cracked open on the burning bitumen. I watched in awe as her transparent and tattered ears flapped gently. There was a slowness and presence in her aura, a calmness I had lost. Elephants have a powerful maternal instinct and will do anything to protect their family, plus they are highly intuitive. I felt like she knew me. I was so close to this magnificent creature that I could see every dry sagging wrinkle and long lashes behind her soulful brown eyes. The hairs on my arm raised in gratitude.

A small wooden stool was placed by the mahout (the keeper of the elephants), near Samba's feet, and one by one, Samba gently lifted each foot onto the stool. She knew the drill. The mahout hosed and vigorously scrubbed her feet, ready for her foot bath and then she gently walked to the large shallow cement bath, where she would stand and soak, whilst munching on bamboo. The next five days, I was able to observe the elephants in their natural environment, aiding in measuring their circumference, which was to ensure they were in a healthy weight range, and was recorded by the staff. Mahouts would stay in the jungle for days and nights. These young men would ensure the elephants were safe; they bathed and cared for them. It was a special bond.

On the second last day, around 3.30pm, six other volunteers and I jumped in the 4WD truck with buckets of paint, paint brushes, gloves and lots of drinking water. We were informed that we would be giving the local school a fresh coat of paint. Once we reached the school grounds, the truck meandered over dried yellow grass, a sand pit and three old car tyres were lined up next to the school house. The corrugated iron barely hung onto the dark, decaying wooden frame, with Cambodian words written down the side. Most of the kids had gone home, except for three young girls who were playing. They grabbed an old tyre each, all of them struggled to roll it, and Once upright, the tyre was at shoulder height. Bare feet and white singlets dashed with giggles over dried grass and red dirt patches.

The aim was to grab as many tyres and roll them with all their might and line them up. I assumed they were waiting for their parents to collect them. I turned my attention to the main classroom. The room was dark, and snippets of light shone through the cracks in the timber walls. The red dirt floor and twelve white wooden tables and chairs were splattered in earthy tones of mud, scuffed by the simplicity to learn.

Jason and his partner Nicky had been to the school earlier in the week, so they navigated the rest of us. Jason asked me to grab a tin of paint, so I picked up my four-litre tin and headed into the classroom.

I hadn't prepared for painting a classroom in my journey to Cambodia, so I just wore the oldest clothes that I had brought to throw out.

"Are you ok to start down the other end, standing on the chair?" said Jason.

"Yep, all good," I replied.

I felt a great sense of humility as I carefully painted the walls of this primitive, almost ancient classroom. Outside was Nicky. I walked out to get some air and noticed what Nicky was doing. She had transformed rotting timber panels into a bright blue sky, with a tree as a sign of life and love being the centrepiece. Brown trunks branched off into puffs of green that surrounded the two square holes representing windows. She put her brush down; it was getting late.

"I think that is it for the day, this is a work in progress," she yelled out. We all packed up and headed back for dinner. As we drove away, I took a deep breath in and gave thanks to the universe for the day.

I am so lucky, I am grateful to have this experience.

The bus ride home was quiet. No one spoke. Perhaps we were all reflecting on our lives back home, and the energy we put into this little school in the most primitive part of Cambodia I had seen.

The next day was our final, and in the morning, I met Mae Ning, one of the most troubled elephants among the other four. She had been rescued from abuse, malnourishment and dehydration after her previous owners overworked her, logging and transporting goods tirelessly for many years. She was blind in one eye and frightened in her new environment. It took time for Mae Ning to gain strength, and once she did, she became a loved member of the herd.

On the 10th February, 2018, I left the elephants with a longing to revisit one day. I felt grounded and clear. I now understood the complications of life back home, the complexities that I had chosen. The stories of the elephants and their gentle aura taught me about trust and learning to reconnect. I now had to face all the thorniness of my life, my fear of really saying goodbye to Daniella, and my fear of embracing Tarni.

Once back at the office and as soon as I had reception, I noticed five missed calls, staring at 6.09am. It was Papa. I felt angry now, like such an idiot. By 7.10am, I had seven missed calls. At 8.26am, my orange Nokia rang again, and I hung up. Four minutes later, it rang again. Furious, I hung up again. I decided to text.

"What do you want?" There was no response.

I grabbed a tuk-tuk and headed to my next stop, a clean and tidy hotel room with a hot shower. 4.11pm and the orange Nokia rung again. I answered this time.

"It's me, Papa. You ready to play Mr Lim in Siem Reap? We need you to get $20,000," he said.

"There is no way I will be playing again," I said.

"Oh, so you forfeit game?" Papa replied.

"Yes," I said, and quickly hung up.

Now that I had an internet connection, I did a quick Google to check out scams in Cambodia. One of the top ten was a gambling scam:

"A tourist will often be approached by a friendly local who asks where they are from. When you tell them, they claim to have knowledge of your country. This is where an invitation

for dinner comes in. A gambling game will usually be going on, which you are invited to play, and of course, lose. Often, visitors may be held at knife point if they refuse to play".

I closed my eyes and remembered Samba and Mae Ning. I recognised my anger and shame and allowed it to pass, sending love to Papa and his family. There was no point in being angry.

What is done is done. I am just lucky to be alive.

20

Reality bites

I returned home to Australia filled with clarity and stillness, yet I just didn't feel well. Tarni collected me from the airport and suggested we have a drink with Bella. It was unusual for me to say no to a glass of wine, but I turned down drinks and went back home, where I still lived with Daniella and went straight to bed. Daniella came home from work. We were both happy to see each other.

"Are you ok, Linda?" she asked, her tone concerned.

"Yes, I think I have a virus or something," I replied.

As the first couple of days passed back in Australia, I felt nauseous and just wanted to sleep. I attempted to go to work on the counselling lines, but had to call in sick just a few hours later. By Sunday, four days after I'd gotten home, my body was aching beyond any flu I had ever had.

Daniella was home in five minutes, and we got in the car. I could feel myself wanting to sleep. We arrived at the Emergency department.

"I'll be fine, just drop me off," I said.

"No way. I'll park the car, see you in there," Daniella said.

I walked into the Emergency department and saw people in the waiting room. I remembered presenting at the counter. The nurse said something that made me realise she knew I was coming. I cannot recall what she said. Daniella was standing next to me.

"Can you take the zipper off my phone?" I said.

I was placed on a bed in the foyer of the Emergency Department. I looked at my hands and noticed they were discoloured, a little purple. That's the last thing I remember.

***

According to an infectious disease expert, for travellers who have been in malarial areas, fever should be considered malaria until proven otherwise. A delay in diagnosis leads to a delay in treatment, which increases the risk of disease progression and complications.

The Centre for Disease Control and infection (CDC)

states that severe malaria occurs when infections are complicated by serious organ failures or abnormalities in the patient's blood or metabolism. The manifestations of severe malaria include:

1. Cerebral malaria, with abnormal behaviour, impaired consciousness, seizures, coma or other neurologic abnormalities
2. Severe anaemia due to Hemolysis (destruction of red blood cells)
3. Acute respiratory distress syndrome, an inflammation reaction in the lungs that inhibits oxygen exchange, which may occur even after the parasite count has decreased
4. Abnormalities in blood coagulation
5. Low blood pressure caused by cardiovascular collapse
6. Acute kidney injury
7. Hyperparasitemia, where more than five per cent of the red blood cells are infected by malaria parasites

I woke up to a high-pitched buzzing, screaming and grunts of pain. I opened my eyes gingerly.

Where am I? Have I been abducted?

I could see what looked like Thunderbird characters in the distance, with large foreheads, straight black fringes, bulging eyes, and robotic movements. I hated them as a child; they scared me. I looked down, every inch of my body was hooked up, plugged in and being monitored by various machines. The thunderbirds hovered around a large square unit attached to the wall, which had Chinese writing on the front.

I really have been abducted.

I yelled out in pain, not really sure why I was in pain. The thunderbirds came rushing in, yet as they got closer, I could see they were wearing NSW Health uniforms, blue scrubs.

"Shelley, are you ok?" a thunderbird asked.

"Who are you?" I asked abruptly.

"My name is Sarah, one of the ICU nurses looking after you. You have been in a coma for five days, Shelley. You were in multi-organ failure, and we are keeping you comfortable with ketamine and other IV drugs and fluids," she said.

My hands. I remember my hands.

They were now even more purple in colour, especially around the first joints. My mouth was very dry. My lips felt cracked. I couldn't get out of bed. An hour later, Daniella, Tarni, Toni, Jules and Eleni arrived. Their warm faces looked down at me, and Tarni and Daniella started to massage my hands.

"We knew you would pull through; nothing keeps my Shell down, " said Jules.

A doctor came around for observation and explained the situation.

"You had two hundred and forty-seven thousand parasites in your body, and a deadly strain of malaria, Malaria Falciparum."

"Oh! Will I be able to run again?" I asked.

"No, Shelley, I doubt you will ever run again."

My heart sank, but I was too drugged and tired to ask much more.

* * *

A few days later, both my hands and feet became increasingly mottled, showing a deeper shade of purple. The pain was excruciating. I wondered where Dad was. Just as I thought it the ICU nurse turned to Tarni and Daniella.

"Does anyone know where Shelley's family is?"

"This is it. We are all her family," Tarni said, pointing at Daniella, Toni, Jules and Eleni.

"Her father lives in Sydney and can't come, and her mother is deceased," Tarni said.

Toni had left her South American Holiday, leaving her partner behind, as the doctors had told Tarni and Daniella that I only had a 20 per cent survival rate. Toni had moved in with Daniella.

Maybe Dad can't come because it would interrupt his

routine of going to the club and drinking? Could Alice not get him in the car with a few roadies?

I fell asleep.

21

Getting Home

Pain: such a short, dull, clipped word to represent a magnitude of discomfort, distress, and so very alone with the deepest, darkest feelings of inadequacy.

Now in a single bed ward with a continual flow of high doses of pain relief such as Endone, Targin, Gabapentin and Fentanyl patches, I watched in shock and fascination as the purple thick skin began to peel off my hands, like a thick rubber glove. The pain was excruciating.

One day, a new doctor appeared by my bedside.

"Shelley, I will have to remove your fingers and toes," he said in a matter-of-fact manner.

"We will have to wait, though," he continued. "We need

your fingers and toes to demarcate."

"What does that mean?" I asked.

"Well, basically, the black dying flesh will start to separate from the viable flesh. This will give us an indication of where to cut, and this way we will hopefully save as much of your fingers and toes as we can. We just have to wait," he replied.

The renal surgeon informed me that I might spend the remainder of my life on a dialysis machine, as my kidneys were unable to function independently. I communicated to Tarni that I would prefer not to live under those circumstances. I had specialised surgeons for so many parts of my body, ranging from foot, hand, kidney, to the heart and blood doctors.

I spent the next eight weeks in the hospital, undergoing dialysis sessions lasting five hours each and receiving twenty units of blood in an attempt to restart my kidneys. Tarni and Daniella were by my side every day. The phone next to my bed and my mobile rang nonstop; most of the calls were from Dad, yet I couldn't answer the phone unless someone was there to help me. One day, I looked at Tarni and finally asked, "Do you know why Dad can't come here?"

"He just said he can't do it. He can't see you like this, and Alice told me that I didn't know your father, and if I did, I would understand," Tarni replied.

***

Hours on the couch led me to a keen desire to research amputations, and I stumbled across some TED Talks by Aimee Mullins, a woman born as a bilateral amputee, and the first woman to be fitted for prosthetic legs, "cheetah legs" shaped with a bouncy type hook at the end so she could run.

In one of her talks, she had researched the word 'disabled' in the thesaurus, and said it meant crippled, helpless, useless, wrecked, stalled, maimed, wounded, mangled, lame, mutilated, run-down, worn out, weakened.

I could relate to worn out and wrecked. My fingers and toes were getting ready to say goodbye; only necrotic tips were left. The toes were often infected, leading to washouts under general anesthesia. I could only imagine that if I were in the wild, like an animal, they would naturally drop off. I missed being in the hospital; it had become my safe place, and the realisation of my lack of independence was paramount. I desperately wanted to get out of the house, yet that meant a shower and a bra. Up until now, the nurses at the hospital had done this.

Toni was an emergency nurse and set up a chair in the shower. I couldn't get my hands and feet wet, as it would make them soggy and prone to infection. I felt vulnerable and helpless just like the thesaurus described.

"Come on, it's nothing I haven't seen before," said Toni, grabbing the sponge. I sat awkwardly on the plastic chair, feet hanging out and arms in the air as instructed.

"Lift your head. It's okay," Toni said, as she gently washed my skinny, limp, naked body.

Tarni was coming to the house at any chance she could. Tarni was also a nurse, and Daniella and Tarni had put their differences aside to care for me. They both loved me very much, and I loved them too, and everything just softened in those moments. Living with Daniella had its ups and downs, and in our most vulnerable moments, we spoke about the ending of our relationship.

"Linda, I'm so sorry, this is all my fault, the fact you you had to leave and then got malaria, I'm just so sorry."

Daniella placed her hands over her face and cried. I placed my hand on her shoulder, and this time I allowed the grief to envelop me. We both looked at each other through blurry tears. Daniella sobbed.

"No, I have my part to play. I'm sorry for the way I left things. It was just a fucking mess, and I felt alone in our relationship. I felt I was gasping for air, and I'm sorry for leaving you the way I did, and now this, I am so so sorry."

We both cried silently until we could face each other through the blur of tears and hurt.

"I'm just so glad you didn't die. I couldn't lose you twice. We will still be friends, won't we?" said Daniella.

"I'm not so convinced that I want to be alive, but I think we've been through a lot and we will be much better as friends," I said with absolute honesty and a knowing deep inside that Daniella would always be in my life.

PART TWO

EAGLE CROSSES THE SUN

22

A new sensation

Not long after Toni showered me, Daniella came home from work, and Tarni popped over for a glass of wine. We all sat down on the couch.

"You probably won't remember, but we have a video of you waking up from a coma," said Tarni.

"Oh, really? No, I don't remember. Show me," I replied.

Tarni pulled out her phone and pressed play.

It was Mia, a friend from Sydney, singing 'Man in the Mirror' by Michael Jackson to me while I was in the Intensive Care Unit. I love this song, and I used to beg Mia to sing it for me whenever I could. The last time she sang it was the night Mum died at the 50th party in Byron Bay. I look at the phone and can see Mia singing, her voice is angelic and powerful. My eyes are closed, and Toni, Jules, Tarni and Daniella are huddled around my bed. There wasn't a lot of standing room between my bloated body, airway tubes, heart monitor, bags of fluid, and the rest of the equipment needed to keep me alive. Tarni held my purple hands, and they all started crying as my head started to move in a gentle nodding motion. I was trying to sing along, and as the chorus hit, 'Take a look at yourself and make a change," my friends belted out the words.

My head moved with all I could muster from side to side as I desperately tried to get the words out: 'Na-na-na, nana-nana.' Tears sprang to my eyes in surprise as I watched the phone. Even in a coma, this song and the love I was surrounded by had been there for me.

Not a day went by without a friend visiting, and Jules, Eleni and Toni started a GoFundMe campaign, which received a great deal of support and extra cash to help cover the medical expenses.

My feet needed constant attention, wrapped in bandages, and a protective 'moon' shoe on each foot was the style. My toes and fingers were dead, not yet amputated, and I was dosed up on copious amounts of drugs. The bandages needed to be changed regularly. I was facing a whole new set of issues in the trail of the deadly mosquito: broken fingers, broken toes, and a broken relationship. I had learnt another lesson the hard way: we cannot run away from our problems geographically – they will always find us and make us face them.

May 4, 2019, I weaned myself off all the hard pain medications, the Fentanyl patches, the Oxycodone, and Gabapentin, all of which were either used for pain, or in the case of Gabapentin, the treatment of neuropathic pain. I decided I would rather feel the numbness and nerve pain in my fingertips than be unable to function without wanting to sleep all the time. Each fingertip has more than 3,000 touch receptors and is considered the most sensitive skin area on the human body. Getting off the drugs left me feeling depressed and anxious. My big concern was being a burden on my partner and friends. My new way of experiencing life involved asking for help to withdraw my card from the ATM, needing assistance with getting dressed, and hiding my hands. Brene Brown says, 'Vulnerability is the most accurate way to measure courage.' I didn't feel courageous; I felt useless.

Once my fingers and toes were amputated, I moved out of my home with Daniella and into a unit with Tarni.

The unit we shared looked out onto the Brunswick Heads River. The water sparkled its magic with intense green and blue hues. It was a healing and peaceful place. I felt held and nurtured. I also felt a deep sense of shame for leaving Daniella. Sitting down at my dining table, I placed my right hand on a blank page in my leather-bound journal, the one Tarni had given to me. She had written a note at the back: 'To beautiful Shell, hope this journal brings new memories! Stories of empowerment and new experiences, your little book of firsts. I adore you.'

I grabbed a pen and carefully drew the outline of my left hand. My right hand is the only one with a joint, and the rest are solid stumps, puckered at the ends where the stitches held the skin together. I can angle the pen to circumnavigate the fat, stumpy ends. Through a raw, dirty, gritty lens, I watched the ink trace what is left of my fingers. I walked away and poured myself a large glass of Pinot Gris. I wrote my first impression: Disfigured, ugly, exposed.

I sipped my wine, and then I wrote something unexpected: 'It is what it is. Capable, courageous.'

Maybe it is the wine talking? I'm not really courageous, but I am capable, though.

I started to research the word touch, and this is what I found:

"On a physical level, pressure receptors are stimulated, which helps lower stress hormones. Emotionally, touching helps make people feel safer and more secure with each other, and when it comes to romantic partnerships, it's an essential indicator that the bonds are healthy and strong."

It is one of the senses we rely on. I had lost the sensation of touch, like someone losing partial vision. The nerve endings were so tingly, the pain would sometimes make my eyes water.

'LOOK AT MY HANDS
LOOK AT THEM
LOOK HARDER
WHAT DO YOU SEE?
DO YOU SEE WHAT I SEE?
I SEE STUMPS
FAT UGLY STUMPS
OR IS IT A CHILD-LIKE HAND THAT DROPS AND SPILTS AGAINST ITS WILL
TOUCH YOUR LOVER WITH YOUR FINGERTIPS
FEEL IT, EMBRACE IT
IT'S SENSUAL, ITS CONNECTION
MY CALLOUSES KEEP ME SAFE FROM HARM
THEY ARE MY PROTECTION
WHAT CAN YOU FEEL?
WHAT DO YOU FEEL?
DO YOU FEEL THE WARMTH OF YOUR PARTNER, YOUR FRIEND, YOUR CHILD

SHELLEY HILL

    HOLD THEIR HAND, PLACE IT IN YOURS
    GRAB YOUR CHILD'S HAND AS THEY WALK ACROSS THE STREET
    AID YOUR MOTHER, YOUR FATHER
    AS YOU GUIDE THEM TO THEIR SEAT
    TAKE MY HAND
    HOLD IT
    I'LL HOLD YOURS
    CAN YOU FEEL ME?
    MY PALM CAN FEEL YOU
    THE REST CAN ONLY IMAGINE WHAT THEY USED TO KNOW
    THE SENSE OF TOUCH IS POWERFUL
    IT'S US, IT'S CONNECTION, IT'S LOVE.

23

You don't have a missing leg

"In the absence of belonging there is suffering,"
- Brene Brown.

My pesky mosquito had come to teach me. Her bite was so deep, her filthy, grotty syringe drew more than just blood. Most of us hate mosquitoes, and I hated myself. Unemployed, vulnerable and disabled. How could I survive whatever might lie ahead and remain in total control? I was calm and determined on the outside, moving on undeterred by such a change in circumstances, the same motto I had held when entering the Police

Academy. My whole existence had been a brave face and a stoic one. Don't feel, don't speak. So naturally, when people asked me, "How are you going?" I replied, "I'm fine." I was not fine. I felt out of place. I felt alone. I had failed at trying to be invisible.

I poured another glass of wine to have with my lunch. I placed the rounded edge of a spoon underneath the ring of my tin of tuna. I lifted the ring, then swiftly turned the spoon around so that I had a lever. I placed the arm of the spoon through the ring. I pulled so the tin was partially open. My next move was to put the stump of my little finger through the middle of the ring; it was the only part that would fit. I pulled it back as I held the tin close to my body for stability. Once opened, the oil spilled down my shirt. I burst into tears and surrendered, slumping over the kitchen bench. I was dancing with the devil, the perfectionist, the 'I'm ok mate, I'll be fine,' version of me.

We pay a price for 'sucking it up'. Our emotional tank gets depleted, and our physical body becomes rigid, equivalent to my fingers and toes, hardened and devoid of any life force. I found myself in an ever-evolving space of 'What do I have to offer?' I was no longer a whole person.

A few months later, and after a lot of googling, I signed up for a one-day course in Brisbane, just two hours away, with a group of amputees. It was hosted by a company called Limbs for Life, which appeared to do some great work for amputees. They were running a workshop for amputees to assist other people, mainly in the hospital setting, to deal with life after trauma and losing a body part. I walked into the sterile conference-type room attached to a motel on a main road. I took a seat and nervously introduced myself to the two women beside me.

"Hi, I'm Shelley," I said.

I could see their eyes scanning my body for a missing limb. Any arms? Legs? Nope, nothing missing that they could see. I looked at the lady next to me, a bilateral amputee, two legs gone. I strategically placed my hands on my desk so she could see. I felt like I didn't belong. I looked around to see the room full of people with missing limbs, mainly legs. My situation and loss immediately feel so insignificant. A young girl from the Gold Coast sat two seats down. She looked fit and tanned, and she also had two missing legs. We all talked about our amputations, and she began to tell her story of being run over and crushed by a bus. In that moment, I felt fortunate that I had all my limbs. The presenter, also with a missing leg, interjected in the discussion.

"Thank you all for coming, and the main purpose of today is to help counsel others who have recently had a limb amputated. Most of our work is in the hospitals, we place our pamphlets in the wards and encourage the nursing staff to refer us to patients that might need someone to talk to."

I felt a little more relaxed now, since counselling others has been a big part of my career. We broke into groups and practised counselling each other with scenario cards and cues, which generally ended in storytelling. I couldn't relate; I didn't have a missing limb. Maybe my lesson was to sit in gratitude; I was still classed as disabled, so I figured I had that in common.

During the lunch break, most of the men and women start talking about stump pain, and the different compression stockings they use to prevent friction on the prosthetic leg. I was eager to finish the day, and what I took with me was that my hands and feet were not the only things defining me.

I had to accept my fate; I intrinsically knew this. Acceptance is a realm we can choose to live in, yet moments of happiness were lacking for me. My life had changed, and I was changing with it. A few days after the Brisbane event, I saw my GP.

"Have you thought about seeing a therapist?" she said.

"Yes," I replied. Therapy has been one of the best things I have ever done throughout my life. I got my referral and made my first appointment with Teneille. Her office was in a cottage-style house, with white weatherboards, little garden beds to the side and a quaint porch with tiny lights illuminating the freshly painted red doorway. Teneille greeted me with a warm smile, and I followed her to her office. It was cosy, with large glossy green plants and a comfortable chair that I immediately sat in.

"So, what brings you here today, Shelley?" I rubbed my hands; my heart was pounding.

"Well, I caught malaria in Cambodia and had my fingers and toes amputated," I began.

"You have been through a lot. How are you coping?" Teneille asked.

I knew this line, I used it all the time, and it was a significant question to ask.

Here we go… here I am. Face-to-face with someone. Not my first rodeo…

To be honest, I didn't know how I was coping; I was just surviving.

"I'm doing ok, considering," I said, with little conviction.

I found that when I was counselling people, and when I'd had therapy in the past, I could sense a connection or a rapport within the first two sessions. There was a knowing, or a relating. If we talk about empathy, being the ability to walk in another's shoes, then most humans have had human experiences like relationship breakups, death, PTSD, trauma, depression, anxiety, low self-esteem, etc, and we can relate and empathise, as we have had that experience ourselves. If you asked me to 'really relate' to someone with children, childbirth, stillborn, pregnancy, infertility, or even what it feels like having children in your life, I would struggle to 'really' relate. I have no children of my own, nor that I spend regular time with them.

My relationship with Teneille as my therapist was clunky, and although she tried to connect, and I tried too, we just didn't. I would say that counselling someone with twenty amputations was new and foreign for her. I tried googling information and support for people with amputations, and most of the time, it was missing legs and arms. I didn't know how to fit back into society. I was a bit of an anomaly, and I also felt like I had done 'talk' therapy to death. I sought a new approach, one that was unconventional and spiritual.

24

Plant medicine

Two years after the amputations, Daniella suggested I try plant medicine. She'd been doing some healing sessions using it and thought it would benefit me.

After some research, I felt the 'call' and booked into my first Ayahuasca ceremony. My biggest fear was to vomit in front of others, and my misconception was that it would be like LSD, which I had tried once and hated. I embarked on a five-day cleanse; no booze, coffee or gluten, and not much solid food. The day of the ceremony was pretty much a liquid fast. It was an overnight stay, and the dress requirement was all white. Apparently, white clothing has a positive effect on someone's aura and was associated with purity and clarity. I went with Toni and her partner, Leah. The location was set in the hills of the Northern Rivers, NSW. As we all drove through the lush green landscape, my hands trembled and my mind raced. I had no idea of what to expect, except that I might vomit.

We parked our cars in a gravelled area, a sharp turn off the main road. A small group of 12 men and women clad in white mingled around,, waiting for our Shaman to collect us to drive us up the hill into what would be my wildest experience yet.

We abandoned our cars, and I abandoned my expectations. As I walked inside, a cat and a young, soft-spoken woman in white greeted me. She was to become my fairy helper, a spirit of the dead, a fallen angel. High glass windows and doors surrounded the room, with pitched wooden rafters offering vast views of the mountains and the naked sky. I signed in with the others, and Toni handed over the car keys. Dusk was now upon us. I noticed a sunken lounge area with upright cushions placed in a circle. I awkwardly introduced myself to the white people, many of whom were experienced in the healing properties of plant medicine.

Our seats had been allocated. I was sitting next to Toni. I looked around to see a large taxidermy of an owl staring intently into the circle. My scan of the room was quick, but not as precise as usual. Eagles, feathers, drums and candles engulfed us as the daylight softened her eyes, ready for the ceremony to begin. The main Shaman 'smudged' us into the sunken circle, while fairy helpers remained on the periphery. I stood in front of him, my arms outstretched, as he chanted and waved his huge eagle feather around my body, incense burning. From the top of my head to my feet.

"Shooo," he said with his feather, jerking quickly away from my body. He reached my feet, and I took my seat. A box of tissues and a white plastic bucket had been neatly placed to my left. The Shaman asked us all to share our intentions for this ceremony. This was done with a "talking stick," a wooden, hand-carved stick adorned with shells and stones, featuring a large head. Everyone got a chance to share as the stick was passed around to each person. I took hold of the stick, much like an Indigenous version of a microphone. I kept my story short.

I liked to expose my hands and feet early, so that everyone could look and stare, alleviating any surprises.

"Hi, my name is Shelley, I have had my toes and fingers amputated, and I feel like I need some healing."

I passed the talking stick quickly to my left, my hands shaking, my heart racing with the terror of public speaking. By the time introductions had finished, darkness was upon us. We were all invited to take our first cup of the plant medicine, a mixture of various Australian plants and vines.

The vines contain the potent DMT (Dimethyltryptamine), a powerful psychotropic substance, which translates as 'the vine of the death' and 'vine of the soul'. The vine is legal in Australia, but extracting the DMT is not. My Shaman had extensive training, and I trusted in feedback from friends who had sat with him. Ayahuasca is a brown brew with an extremely bitter taste, enough to make some people gag. It commonly causes purging, both physical and psychosomatic, a transformational experience of releasing stuck emotions and energy. This purge can result in vomiting and diarrhoea. A slice of orange was offered after we drank our first cup, due to its disgusting taste. One by one, we sat before our Shaman and drank our brown, revolting tea, desperate for the sweetness of the orange. As we all took our allocated spaces, there was absolute silence, a settling in, a meditation. Moments later, soft music began to play. I started to feel euphoric; a kaleidoscope of purple and orange swirled at my third eye, feeling warm and comforting. For each person, the potent plant will take effect quickly or may take a considerable amount of time. The silence broke as I started to hear a woman to my right. It wasn't Toni. A moaning, a deep guttural moan, and then a scream.

I hope she is ok?

She got louder and louder. In a blur, I opened my eyes and saw the fairies take her outside to the grass. This was a grounding process, on the earth, under the expansive sky of shining stars. At that point, I was quite aware of what was going on. The Shaman started chanting in what sounded like a native South American language. The music got deeper. I could hear men making grunting noises, as if they were in pain. I could sense Toni next to me, rigid and in control, just as though she'd had a cup of chamomile tea. That was Toni, though, always in control. As the music deepened, the plant grabbed hold of my body. Tears streamed down my face, my shoulders started to shudder, and my nose ran like a leaking tap. My breathing was short and sharp, my chest moved like I was having a panic attack, and then in a distinct vision, I saw the black necrotic death of my fingers and toes, shrivelled and ready to be brutally chopped. I sobbed and sobbed, my breathing became longer and slower. I couldn't do anything but go with it.

The room was now filled with sounds of purging, vomiting, groaning, sighing, and a few angry outbursts. The ayahuasca experience was a seven-hour one, from 6pm to approximately 1am. About halfway through, the music slowed down, and we were invited to take a second cup, or three-quarters, or half, or none. A little hazy, I got up and requested half a cup; it didn't taste too bad this time. The fairies started singing different South American lyrics with the Shaman. The music intensified, and I could not stop crying. I was crying so hard that I made noises, a soft whaling in between sobs. My whole body began to slump in absolute grief. The music plays an important role in Aya; we got some patches of relief, and in that, I stopped sobbing. I felt slightly aware of my surroundings and made my way quickly to the downstairs toilet, with diarrhoea. This continuum happened all night. Sobbing, blowing my nose, toilet. As the ceremony started to close, the music softened, and violent vomiting could be heard, the final release. I came to, my body half upright, yet my head was on the floor near my tissue box. Exhausted, with crusty eyes, the tears turned to grit, I opened them and saw the owl staring at me. The fairies gently removed the plastic buckets and tipped all the brown suffering and pain onto the grass outside. The Shaman came around with a cleansing oil for us to smell, to bring us back. Everyone was shattered. We had a cup of tea, a root vegetable soup, and homemade bread to nourish our souls. The area was cleared by the fairies, and we all slept on couches or thin mattresses, covered in our white blankets. It was 2am. Toni and Leah snuggled together.

As daylight cracked, I woke to the open sky and made myself a cup of tea. Each of us had a job of cleaning up. Wash the vomit buckets, vacuum, clean the kitchen and make the sunken lounge into a clean space for the next round of the talking stick, to debrief. I just wanted to go home. I had nothing left. I shared my experience with a short and open explanation.

"I just could not stop crying, and all the grief from the past two years came at me like a tidal wave. I have nothing more to say, I am pretty tired,' I said.

I would never have cried in front of a therapist like I did with Madre. Madre is the Mother Ayahuasca. I started therapy in my 20s, and Aya broke me in a way that felt as though I'd had ten years of therapy in one session. I found it difficult to cry in front of others, and yet the plant gave me this gift, a vulnerable journey, like group therapy with a twist.

I did Aya three times, the second time being on the 2nd February in 2020. My intention was self-love. During my five-day cleanse, leading up to the ceremony, I was coughing a lot with dreams of the police, a recurring dream of fucking up. At my second ceremony, it was so different; I felt the absence of my father. After my second cup, my head was thrown back and forth, to the front of my chest and then to the base of my neck, violently. I was being whiplashed.

"OPEN YOUR VOICE, PEOPLE WANT TO HEAR YOU SPEAK," Madre demanded. With a jerking movement, my head went backwards; no control. My chest rose as I opened to love, communication and spirit.

"Open your throat and roar," Madre said. This went

on for the duration of the journey. Six months later, I completed my third ceremony. My intention was to prioritise myself. A small group of us did it together, including Tarni and Daniella. I didn't sit near them. This time, I had a full second cup. Madre forced me to sit upright. I was focused and still, almost in a meditative space. Nothing around me mattered, and when the chatter in my brain started, Madre would say, "Shut up, Shelley", and I would be present again. An Indigenous man started playing the didgeridoo. I felt a powerful message to stay in my power. The message I received was: "What has been holding me back from prioritising myself is myself, and everything I do is in busyness, and people pleasing."

As my final ceremony closed, I vomited violently into my bucket. There was no nausea; it just came out of me. As I came to my head was slumped in the bucket. I was exhausted with a pounding headache. Aya has been the most profound healing experience to date. I had to be ready and willing.

25

What is resilience

I was determined not to be that person who identified as 'disabled'. I wanted to do everything, and if not more than I had ever done. The clarity of the doctor's words etched in my mind: 'You will never run again, Shelley.' I placed my stumped feet into a pair of runners, my teeth clenched as I recalled the doctor's words. My mosquito energy kicked in, eager to take a bite, determined to draw blood, and step by step, I ran so hard that my feet begged for relief.

I also embarked on a weekly routine of kettlebell classes. My trainer, Pete, was the most inspirational man - a ball of muscle and a gentle soul. I didn't know how to use a kettlebell. As I walked into a class full of experienced kettlebell participants, Pete approached me.

"Hi, my name is Pete. Have you used a kettlebell before?" he asked.

"No," I replied.

"I am not sure how you will hang on, but let's give it a go," he said.

I grabbed my pink coloured 8 kilogram bell by its slightly rusted handle; the rough surface made it easier to grip. I watched Pete with a close eye, trying to get the 'clean and press' right.

"Hold the bell at your side and as the hand moves up towards your chest, keep it close and flick your wrist as the bell lands on your chest, let it rest tight between your shoulders. That's the clean, then push your arm straight up over your head, that's the press," Pete instructed. It was a particular move, and after a few days and many corrections, I was able to do it. We then moved to legs.

"Grab both bells and hold them by your side and step backwards into a lunge," Pete instructed. Balancing with 8 kilograms in each hand, no toes, and half a set of fingers was a mental test of endurance and focus. I became obsessed. I started getting up each day at 5am just for Pete's class. His energy, motivation and my determination to get stronger pushed me to feel "normal again" I was clean and pressing 14 kilograms in each hand and lunging with 18 kilograms on either side. I felt strong and capable.

On top of that, I was running again, not just running, sprinting. I was pushing my body to prove I could do what I used to do. I loved to challenge my body, I love the pain, the sweat, the adrenaline and the endorphin release of exercising.

A visit to Dad and Alice would often end up running up and down the Coogee stairs. The footballers use them for training, and there are approximately 223 steps. Some are very steep, and the payoff at the top was the most spectacular view of the crystal ocean, Wedding Cake Island, and if I were lucky, the giant spurt of a whale passing through would leave me with my cup filled.

On one visit, I snuck out of Dad's house at 5.30am, careful not to wake him and Alice. I made my way to the stairs. The sun was warm, I was exhilarated from the exercise, and on my fifth set of stairs, I saw a young man with a glossy black Labrador by his side. The lab had a vest that said "MIND DOG." I knew this organisation; they helped people who were experiencing mental health issues to train their dogs, which results in easing anxiety and depression in their owners. The young man, his lab, and I were in a dance of who could pass each other first. As we began the dance, he placed his hand out, indicating for me to shake it. I willingly accepted his offer and placed my tiny hand in his. He pulled his hand away in a cautious movement, slow, but not too fast. He looked at my hand and said, "Broken Fingers."

He walked past me with his dog, and I felt somewhat happy about his comment. Often people are too afraid to ask, "What happened?' He didn't need to ask; he was observant, and in his observation, I felt seen. A strange interaction left me smiling as I continued on my way to the expanse of the ocean and sky.

People started calling me resilient. I Googled the word resilience:

"Resilience is the process and outcome of successfully adapting to difficult or challenging experiences, especially through mental, emotional, and behavioural flexibility, an adjustment to external demands and internal demands."

The Oxford dictionary said it meant:
1. The capacity to withstand or recover quickly from difficulties and toughness.
2. The ability of a substance or object to spring back into shape; elasticity. "Nylon is excellent in wearability and resilience".

A friend once said, "We like to use the word resilience a lot, especially when talking about disasters and tragedies."

Living in the Northern Rivers, NSW, where the 100-year floods took place, where the water reached over

15 metres above ground level in Lismore, and homes and lives were destroyed, was a tragedy and a natural disaster. The Widjabul people of the Bundjalung land predicted this and told the white fellas not to build in Lismore.

In 2021, I bought a 1.5-acre property with no neighbours in sight in the hinterland of Byron Bay, where the black squawking cockatoos, the open fire, and the surrounding native trees live. It was a place where Tarni and I could escape and ground. We were 30 minutes from Lismore. I was one of the lucky ones in the floods. People in Lismore, and various other towns spread far and wide, scrambled to their rooftops as the water rose. Their livestock, horses, cows, cats, and dogs floated down the street in murky, gushing water, while brown snakes circled their once-living room. What was left of these people's homes was spewed out onto the street, leaving a pile of their possessions, their heirlooms; pieces of their life they had built to fester in filthy mud until the rain finally stopped. The stench was unbearable. Many were left homeless and had to live in a recreation centre on sleeping bags. Children, babies, rescued dogs, and all walks of life came together in one big room, with food and clothing supplies being delivered daily. Everything was lost. When I looked at the dictionary's version of resilience and the capacity to 'quickly' recover, it felt unrealistic in this situation. Then there is the other quote of "Successfully adapting to difficult and challenging experiences." How could we measure success in a tragedy like this, I wondered.

Was my success based on lunging with no toes, holding 18-kilogram kettlebells on either side? I have no fingers and toes, but I can run again. Does that make me a success? That was my success at the time, and yet the emotional trauma will suppurate in the dark shadows of our being, just like the favourite armchair our grandfather used to sit in, the fabric covered in red mud, its springs broken. That chair will never have the capacity to be as resilient as nylon.

Often, when others are around people who have had great trauma, they feel that they can't talk about their 'little' trauma, because it feels insensitive. Yet what is a 'little' trauma, and how do we measure what is big or little for each person? The fact is, we can't. There is no denying anyone's reality. I don't have a missing limb, or two missing limbs for that matter. I feel lucky, yet my stump pain and nerve damage on twenty digits is just as painful and real as a person with limb loss.

I could call myself resilient. It's messy, and anything is possible, but it's more than just resilience. When life strikes in a way we don't expect, we must make a choice, and it can take time, years, to recover. Acceptance was my choice, and moments of happiness began to emerge. I reminded myself of one significant lesson: Trauma: you can't go under it, you can't go around it, you have to go through it.

Acceptance is spacious.

26

Gray Street

The RSL club in Gray Street, Bondi Junction, was Dad's second home. The fascia, a deep maroon with bold dark blue letters 'CLUB BONDI JUNCTION RSL'. The entrance was dark with a screened smoking corner to the left. By 9am, as soon as the door opened, Dad was at the bar ordering his first schooner of Carlton Draught. The club was located in a busy street, with no real outlook except for parked cars and passers-by rushing to get the bus or do their shopping at Westfield. The carpet was old and smelled like stale beer, and Dad would meet his friends there every day. This was his routine. Alice would drop him off and spend the next three hours wandering around the shops, purchasing items and clothes to soothe her loneliness. Dad could drink a schooner of beer in 15 minutes, so he managed to have at least six before midday. He would often wear his favourite Vietnam Veterans black T-shirt, and a pair of shorts, with his long grey hair tied in a ponytail. Alice was 13 years younger than him, with an endearing Irish accent, soft blonde hair, a small physique, and colourful, groovy outfits that made her feel good. She was always in a hurry, walking fast, no time to take in the moment. Her arms moved vigorously back and forward, like a walker competing in the Olympic Games, feet only just touching the busy shopping mall. I was pretty fast, considering I had no toes and decent shoes, but I couldn't maintain her pace. Dad nicknamed her "The Minister for War." Her tone was often abrupt and ready for a fight, defensive yet friendly, but not warm. Dad didn't have a mobile phone, so Alice would arrive to pick him up after his belly was full of beer, around 12pm, mainly with a classy new outfit from Lululemon.

"Just one more, come and sit with us," he would say. Alice would sometimes reluctantly do this, just to please him, and on occasion, so did I. I hated that place, but it was often the only way I got to see Dad, half tanked and with his next beer in hand. Once he got back home, my father would sit and drink more beer whilst Alice prepared dinner. Each day was the same for years until things changed in 2021.

After drinking 15 beers a day, my father's incontinence progressed, and so did the supply of adult nappies. Alice would gather the soiled nappies and place them in public bins around the Eastern Suburbs. She was too embarrassed to fill the residential bin and could not stand the stench. My father was malnourished, and refused to barely eat a meal, yet the beers kept flowing, and gave him some sort of nutrients, a bit of barley and sugar. On June 6, 2021, around 10pm, I received a call from Alice.

"Your father has fallen out of bed, and I can't get him up, and he can't get up himself, I don't know what to do."

"Maybe call an ambulance," I suggested. Dad was taken to the hospital, and I flew to Sydney the next day.

He had broken his hip and needed an operation. After the operation, the anaesthetic sent him into a delirium, which is a common thing if someone has been a heavy drinker. Walking back into a hospital environment evoked all sorts of memories. Many memories from Mum and my own journey; the smell, the large doors opening into a ward full of sick people, white cotton blankets, and nurses run off their feet, with unequal patient-to-staff ratios. It was odd to see Dad vulnerable, in a hospital bed and talking rubbish.

"Have a go at the guy over there, hoeing into his beer," he said, pointing to another patient who was holding a urine bottle.

The auxiliary ladies had knitted a pink and white teddy,

which was left on the bedside table of an empty bed.

"Hey matey, go and steal that teddy."

I grabbed the teddy and gave it to him; he held it and cuddled it like a little boy. This day was the beginning of his demise. Two weeks passed, and Dad had been moved four times into different rooms. If there is anything I know personally about PTSD, it is that routine and structure keep you sane. My father's demeanour started changing; he became aggressive and agitated, talking about the war.

"Why would they get a young boy to do a man's job?" he started to cry. I didn't know if I had ever seen him cry. I sat next to him on the bed; his hands were trembling.

"I love you, Matey," he said.

This was rare, and in that moment, I felt his pain. I felt the tears well up in my eyes.

"I love you too, Dad," I said, as I gingerly touched his soft, thin hair. I felt connected, and I briefly reflected upon his journey in life. What was it like being called up at 19 to fight a war? To serve his country and not to have recognition when he came home? As a child, I saw and experienced an angry young man returning home from war. He was different, and I was too young to understand or empathise. I moved closer to Dad and leaned towards his hunched, bony shoulders. Bending down to his warmth, I remained there for a few moments longer than planned.

"Hey Matey," he whispered. "I'm sorry I didn't come

and see you in the hospital. I worry about it all the time, I just couldn't."

"It's ok, Dad, I understand."

I had grappled with this grief; it was thick, like black sooty smoke that I had to wade through to gain perspective, a perspective from a Vietnam Veteran. A man who was commissioned to fight a war at the age of 19.

It was a long journey in the hospital for me after Malaria, without a single family member present. Where was Dad? Where was his wife, Alice? My father once told me that he saw many of his comrades in the hospital during the war. His PTSD was evident as his head dropped, now in the hospital himself. His eyes filled with tears. He reached out to hug me. It felt awkward.

"I forgive you, Dad," I said. I held back my own tears now. I wanted them to flow like little streams down my face, but instead they swelled in my eyes and I quickly wiped them away. Dad started talking in riddles until another lucid moment presented itself; he then began to talk about the war again.

"There were 8 Vietnamese women bashing me with bamboo, they wouldn't stop, and I had to steal a bike to get away". That's all I got as his brain flicked back to something random. No one rides for free in this life.

A year later, my father was diagnosed with Alcohol Related Dementia. I began to get curious about the progression of the disease and what to expect. I read this: "When the horror of your mind persists, only madness and dementia can remove it" (unknown author).

Did his soul and mind shut down the horror of the war? What about the trauma from the fire brigade? Did dementia also develop as a means of coping, of not dealing with his pain and suffering? I posed these philosophical questions to myself. In his early stages of dementia, the angry man began to soften, and his ability to walk decreased. He was bound by deep sadness, and for the second time, one of the most profound things he said to me was, "The thing I will most regret is not coming to see you in the hospital. I miss you so much, Matey."

I just softly repeated myself, "I forgive you, Dad."

Those heartfelt words enabled me to see him through a new lens, one of love and compassion. For the last 50 years, we had both survived in detachment, avoidance, and judgment for the mistakes we had both made in the past. Judgement is like abandoning yourself. Why invest so much interest in others when you could be focusing on your own journey? To my surprise, I wanted to be affectionate towards him. I put lip balm on his dehydrated lips and kissed his forehead, then stroked his hair from his forehead slowly with my new hand. The hardened callous tips were unable to feel the sensation of hair, so I touched his hair with my palm instead. I walked away from the hospital feeling a closeness I had never felt between us.

It was different with mum; I was young and frustrated with my role as the caretaker, and I felt alone in the experience. She was also angry and bitterly depressed, a place that was hard to connect with. The lead-up to her death was prolonged and tragic. The feeling with Dad was different, spacious in some way, and my approach to life and death was now one of acceptance. I just had to breathe into a new chapter.

Once Dad returned home from the hospital, he struggled to walk. The club closed down, he lost his friends, his routine, and would lie in bed watching old Western DVDs. He was agitated and developed Parkinson's disease, with his right hand shaking. Increasingly, his cognition declined, and his mobility was poor. It was like walking on eggshells, waiting for him to fall. Alice and I began to put lemonade in his beer; he still drank them as if he were dying of thirst. A few months later, he began to dislike the feeling of being drunk.

"This stuff is knocking me about," he'd say. He stopped participating in life. He didn't want to leave the house, unless it was a doctor's appointment, for hearing aids, a geriatrician or skin checks. Over the next two years, Dad had melanomas removed and a double knee replacement.

Alice didn't want to leave him alone, terrified he would fall. She was at a breaking point and would call me, saying things like, "I feel like I'm standing on the edge of a cliff." Her anxiety was palpable.

My visits to Sydney became more regular. Alice could not manage him at home and started a course of anti-depressants to manage her anxiety; she started smoking again and drinking a lot of champagne each day to cope. She would put her bubbles in coloured flutes, so Dad didn't know what she was drinking.

Dad begged and pleaded not to go into a nursing home. He would be better, he would behave, he would bargain - but it was too late. Alice increasingly became emotionally removed. She was young, attractive, and wanted to live her life, see friends and go places.

My father had a landline portable phone, and he knew if he pressed No.1, he would reach Alice on her mobile, and if he pressed No.2, he would reach me. When he was left alone, he would incessantly press those buttons. Alice would be gone for five minutes, and he would call her.

"When are you coming home?"

Alice was frustrated. "KENNY! I just left. I need some space."

"Ok Matey," he'd reply cheerfully. Five minutes later, he would call again and ask the same question. If Alice didn't answer, he would call me. It was a daily exercise in patience.

Each visit became the same; as soon as I walked through the door, Dad would walk toward me with his arms wide open for a cuddle. He was happy to see me, and it was unusual behaviour. I stood on my tiptoes and reached up to hug him; his beard prickled my face, tickling me, and I laughed, moving out of his embrace. It felt foreign, yet I knew he was genuine. There were lots of hugs and lots of, "I love you, Matey." That was the new dad.

One visit, Alice and I poured ourselves a champers and sat together outside, slumped into the chairs with pure exhaustion and fear of what was to come. Dad wasn't far behind us; he'd picked up the pace on his walker.

"Can I have a drink too?" he said.

"Kenny, you can only have three beers no more, OK!" Alice replied abruptly.

"Very strict around here," he said with a smile. I grabbed Dad a XXXX beer with a dash of lemonade. It's a little lower in alcohol than his previously loved Carlton Draught. Dad got up to wee in the garden, which saved him a trip to the toilet on his walker. He hid around the corner and came back in his blue nappy.

"I'm just going to sit here in my blueys," he said. There was Dad, long grey hair tied in a ponytail, tattoos, no shirt, a nappy, his walker placed by his side with a shandy beer in his hand.

27

The soldier and the battle

In September 2023, the inevitable happened. Dad was to be admitted to his first nursing home, under the provision of respite, with the intention of becoming a permanent resident. The time could not come quick enough for Alice, as she booked her flight back home to Ireland to see family. She told Dad she would be gone for three weeks, yet she never saw him for five. She wanted a 2-week break at home before she left, so I agreed to fabricate some dates and stay at the house and visit Dad. I flew down a day earlier to check out the nursing home with Alice. Leaving Dad alone at home was getting a little risky, since his spatial perception was declining. He would bump into walls with his walker or not use it at all. Alice left three zero-alcohol beers in the fridge. We had jumped in the car seconds before Alice's phone rang.

"Hey Matey, what time will you be back?"

"Kenny! You are driving us nuts, we told you one hour, now stop calling me!" Alice snapped.

"We will be quick, Vaucluse isn't that far," I said gently.

The busy traffic to Vaucluse took us 30 minutes to navigate. Alice exited the car as quickly as she could.

"Come on, Shelley, grab the nappies and photos," she said, already ten paces ahead of me. The outside of the building was dusty pink. It looked like it needed some TLC (tender loving care). We walked up to the black aluminium gate, punched in the provided pin code 1587, and the gate opened to a table full of nasal swabs for COVID. Swab, check, negative, sign in. Another coded door, pin 2083, and we were in. We were met by the manager, who took us on a tour. Alice had already checked the place out and put down a deposit.

"What do you think, Shelley? she asked.

I looked down the narrow corridor and saw a man in a wheelchair, with a crash helmet on, using his feet to manoeuvre himself up and down the cream-coloured lino. His head was tilted down to the left as he made grunting noises.

"Come on, Peter, let's go," one of the nurses coaxed. I felt overwhelmed.

"It is fine, Alice. Let's have a look at Dad's room."

We walked down the long corridor. I looked to my left and noticed a woman in her room, pale, alone, asleep, curtains drawn.

Is she palliative?

My next encounter was the 'Clapper'. The 'Clapper' was a small-framed woman with loose grey pants and a stained white t-shirt to match. She appeared to be a very cheery old woman, approaching us and clapping her hands continuously. I nodded and smiled. Word from the nursing staff was that she was a teacher in her younger years. We entered Dad's new room. It was huge, with too many chairs, and the bathroom was far away from the bed. This was where he was to spend the next five weeks or longer.

Alice made conversation with a young man who was cleaning the room. I couldn't wait to get out of there. I poked my head out of Dad's new room, and saw two women arm in arm, like best friends. One of them looked cranky, with an intense frown. I tried to walk back into Dad's room, but they came closer and closer. I smiled and waved my right hand at the cranky one, as she seemed to be the leader of the pair. She launched forward, grabbing my wrist.

"You don't belong here, get out, you don't belong here, go away!"

I felt frightened. She released her grip, and a young staff member walked quickly towards us down the hall.

"Sorry!" she said. "That's Norma, she doesn't like new people."

Alice started shoving the nappies in a drawer and placing photos around. We left in a hurry, wanting to get home to Dad. I suggested we grab a bottle of champagne to take home.

"I think we need one Shelley, it's okay that place… isn't it?" Alice asked, fumbling to find some cash to buy the champagne.

"Yeah, yeah, it's totally fine for now, you just focus on your holiday, I'll visit Dad," I replied.

We got back to the house. Dad was happy to see us and opened his arms for a cuddle. We popped the champagne in the fridge and noticed the three beers were gone. He may not have known what day it was, but he certainly remembered that there were three cold beers in the fridge. Alice and I looked at each other with knowing eyes. Tomorrow, Dad would no longer be sitting in his own backyard enjoying a beer, or sleeping next to his wife, or being familiar with his surroundings. The champagne bottle was finished quickly, and Dad was on his 6th zero beer.

The next day, we all got up early and packed Dad,

his walker, clothes, western DVDs, a few zero alcohol beers, his favourite rum and raisin chocolate, blueberries, yoghurt, ice cream and the old transistor radio into the little silver two-door Suzuki. I squeezed in the back next to the wheelie walker, with a few spare urine bottles, and off we went to Dad's new home.

Dad knew he was going into care, but he thought it was short-term. Just for three weeks so Alice could see her family. Pin code 1587. COVID-19 swab, negative, pin code 2083. The automatic doors closed quickly behind us.

"Gaday love," my dad said to the manager. Dad attempted to make silly jokes about her dyed red hair.

"Come on, Kenny, let's go and see your room," Alice said, trying to get his attention.

The Clapper saw us walking towards her and clapped excitedly. Dad thought this was fun and clapped back.

"Hi, Love, how ya goin'?"

The Clapper ignored him and walked past us with the same outfit on as yesterday. Her eyes were vacant. The Clapper followed us to Dad's room. She was on her way to the morning tea trolley; she loved the Monte Carlos and shortbread creams. The kitchen was near Dad's room. My father sat down in his choice of four chairs. Alice and I rushed around placing his clothes in the drawers. There was a little bar fridge in his room, where we placed his 000 beers and cold food.

"Come on, Kenny, let's have a walk," Alice said. Dad got hold of his walker and headed towards the front door, bumping into walls.

"No, this way, Dad, let's go outside," I said, guiding his walker in the opposite direction. We had to pass the kitchen to gain access to the garden.

Oh no, there is the woman outside that grabbed me, Norma!

She looked up and smiled, and said hello this time. Clearly, I wasn't that "new" today. The garden was well-maintained. Australian Native plants and grasses were neatly placed amongst the grey pavers, making it easy access for wheelie walkers to get to the undercover sitting area. The nursing home was located in a high-density living area. Unit blocks surrounded the garden, with balconies and windows facing onto us as we tried to settle Dad in.

"Let's sit here, Kenny," Alice said, as we both directed Dad from his walker into a sturdy outdoor chair.

"Remember, Kenny, right hand down first," Alice said nervously.

Dad plonked down, only just making a connection with the chair.

"I'm coming home with you both, right? You aren't leaving me here?" he asked. His face tightened with fear; his right hand shaking so hard he had to grab it with his left hand.

"Please, don't leave me here."

At this stage of his dementia, he was partially conscious enough to understand what was happening.

"It is just a short time, while I go and see my son, Rian. He is getting married in Ireland, remember Kenny? I said it so many times," Alice's voice was high-pitched and frustrated.

Dad could not remember recent conversations or what month it was, and would laugh and nod as if he knew what we were talking about. He didn't have many words to say; he wasn't a man of many words to begin with. A few minutes later, we all went back to Dad's room.

"Now, Shelley, you will have to make sure his hearing aids are charged whilst I'm away," Alice said in a stern tone. I nodded, wondering how I would get the tiny little buds into the charger with my stumpy half fingers.

It was now time to leave, to beat the school traffic and have a glass of champagne. This had become a ritual, a habit, a time to debrief. As Alice and I walked down the corridor, nurses rushed from room to room, buzzers sounding and the Clapper clapping. Dad followed us with his walker. We got to the front door, he stopped, he waved us goodbye, calm with a sense of knowing perhaps. Leaving him there broke my heart. He turned slowly back towards his room, his tall frame hunched over his walker, navigating the Clapper, crash helmet Peter, and Norma.

It reminded me of a note I wrote all those years ago in one of my Buddhism classes: 'A patient mind accepts and deals with what life throws at us.'

"See you tomorrow, Dad," I called as I entered code 2083. My shoulders dropped, I held my breath and sighed. That was one of the hardest things I have had to do.

A week later, Alice flew to Ireland. She splurged and flew business class, with a new wardrobe and a set of expensive matching luggage. Dad would have hit the roof knowing she was using his money in such an extravagant way. She deserved a splurge, and she felt good about her appearance. I stayed at the house with Tarni and our dog Nibbles, where we packed a daily bag of homemade sandwiches, yoghurt, berries and a ration of chocolate; otherwise Dad would eat the entire block. I felt a sense of purpose and freedom from Alice's anxious energy. I visited Dad almost every day, and every day he would ask me when Alice was coming home. Every day I lied and told him three weeks, when it was really five. By week three, he became angry.

"This is bullshit! She has left me here, hasn't she?"

"No, Dad, she is coming home. And remember your mate Lumpy (a bikey mate) came to see you the other day?" I coaxed, trying to change the conversation.

Dad just seemed unhappy most of the time and would eat his meals alone in his room. He wasn't as 'bad' as some of the other residents, yet it was a matter of urgency to get him placed in care, so that Alice could leave the country.

We would sit in the garden, I would watch as he grabbed handfuls of blueberries, a bite of a sandwich, some chocolate, and then back to the berries. He shoved this in his mouth and filled it up to capacity, and then wanted to talk. I had never heard Dad talk so much.

"Dad, I can't understand you with your mouth full," I would say. This dialogue was done with repetition. He loved his food and never requested a beer. Two weeks into his stay, a UTI infection sent him into another delirium. I never knew this was possible, but that is what happened. His room began to smell of urine, and he would urgently drop his daks (pants) in the garden of the nursing home. He smashed all the pictures in the hallway. The police were called, and he was taken to the hospital overnight for an assessment. Once back at the nursing home, he became quite depressed. He lost interest in the sandwiches I made him and started to point at objects or people that weren't there. Every now and then, he had a lucid moment.

"It was the bloody grog, that's why I'm here."

Tarni and I took Nibbles to the nursing home; Dad loved to touch his soft doodle fur. Nibbles had just been desexed, and Dad called him 'No balls.'

His favourite comment to make was, "He has no balls, and you have no toes, I think we will all get on fine."

Once Alice arrived home, she wanted to move Dad closer to their house, so within three months, Dad moved to another nursing home. It was within walking distance of his house, with a bright, sunny room. He made friends with a couple of the older men, as they would sit and eat each meal together, pretending to understand the conversation. It was a high-care dementia unit. When I came to Sydney, Alice and I would take Dad home on the weekend for a swim in the pool. Most of the time, he was naked, and it didn't bother him to eat his lunch nude in front of his daughter. It was a little confronting for me, so I would throw a towel on his lap. He was able to lie down in his own bed and be in his own home most weekends for about a month until his mobility declined even further, along with his proprioception. That was about the time he stopped telling me he loved me each visit.

28

Death

*"When someone dies, and it's a beautiful death,
in that there is no ego, there is no struggle. They let go
of the ego. In this peace is joy, love and happiness."
12/5/2010, The Meditation Space, Surry Hills, Sydney.*

Dr Roger Cole, a palliative care doctor, talked about life, death, attachment, ego, forgiveness and love from a spiritual position. He wrote a book called "Mission to Love." I will never stop reading over these notes, a reminder of what truly matters. 'Forgiveness liberates us from the sorrow of the past, and frees us from the pain that memory causes. When someone dies a beautiful death, there is no ego, no struggle. They let go of the ego. In that peace is joy, love and happiness.'

What do we know about death? The pain for loved ones left behind? For some, there might be relief after a prolonged period of dementia or cancer. Is it tragic or is it sudden?

I have always been curious about death and the life that encapsulates the soul before it passes on. When I was in the police, I saw a lot of death, from motor vehicle accidents, suicide, natural causes, to horrendous crimes resulting in murder from a domestic violence incident. Many people would strategically plan their suicide, as routine as getting up each day and going to work. Leaving a note, or folding their clothes in a particular way, planned and ready to be found by someone who cares, someone who may never get that vision out of their mind; a loved one hanging from the rafters in the family garage, or the person so determined that they would jump off a cliff and land in the ocean allowing the creatures below to feast on human flesh.

We are all going to die, that is a fact, and a process. Elizabeth Kubler Ross, a well-known Swiss American Psychiatrist who wrote a book called "On Death and Dying," describes the five stages of grief as: denial, anger, bargaining, depression and acceptance. From my own experience, these don't necessarily go in that order.

How does someone deal with a diagnosis of cancer, for

example? Is it denial and anger as the first emotion, or does someone accept their fate and then go through the other processes? Our fate is meant to teach us, yet we don't know why until years later, or we never know why. Why does the woman with three children and a loving relationship have six months to live? How do we grasp this reality? What if you found your daughter dead in her room at thirty-nine years old from an unknown heart condition? Suddenly, you are left to raise her two children in your later years of life, as my father's sister was.

What was it really like for my loved ones seeing me in a coma, not knowing the outcome? I know what that is like after witnessing my mother's decline. It is all-consuming, scary and anxiety-provoking; leaving my phone beside my bed, waiting for 'the call'.

Watching my father struggle with dementia was more painful than seeing him palliative. Visits to the nursing home, watching him urinate in corners, with limited perception of his whereabouts. Difficult and repetitive conversations were exhausting, and finding Dad lying on his bed, his hand shaking, alone and waiting to die, was confronting. Six months after his long-term stay at the new nursing home, his two friends, Don and Eric, died. I hoped my father would soon let go of this world and be at peace, and I know he wanted that too.

During our last conversation, he said, "Hey Matey, how old am I? And when is a good time to die? Your dad is fucked."

I touched his frail hands and said, "Dad, you are 78, and you let go when you are ready. No one thought you would make it this long."

We both smiled.

A week later, he fell and fractured five ribs, and one week after that, I got the 'call' from Alice.

"Your father has had another fall and hit his head. He has a bleed to the brain; he is palliative, Shelley."

Tarni and I flew to Sydney the next day.

We entered the Acute Services building at Prince of Wales Hospital in Randwick. Dad was in bed number 11. Number 11 has significance for me. I was born on November 11, Daniella was born on June 11, my mother died on May 11, and my grandmother passed on August 11.

The room was dimly lit, and I noticed the tree of life symbol on his door. Alice was holding his hand, with tears in her eyes. Dad was struggling to breathe, mainly due to the fractured ribs. His red and yellow inked Vietnam tattoo was covered in bruises, and his right eye was also bruised from the fall. Dad had one other tattoo on his shoulder; this one was intact. I recalled a memory of him holding me in the air; we were in the ocean, and there was a smile on my 2-year-old face. This other tattoo was faded with age and a sign of wisdom. It was an eagle crossing the sun. His once-muscular physique was gaunt and bony, and his feet were jammed up against the end of the hospital bed. There was not a bed long enough for his lofty height. I sat next to him and squeezed his hand.

"Hey, Dad, it's me." He squeezed my hand as tight as he could and let out a deep sigh. I cried. This was the end.

Tarni whispered in his ear, "Hey, Kenny, we love you."

Daniella sent me a text: "How is he?"

"He is dying," I replied.

"Can I speak to him?" she said.

"He won't be able to respond, but I'll hold the phone close to his ear," I texted.

She rang.

"Hey, Kenny, it's me, Daniella. Remember the fun we had shooting beer cans in your garage and drinking beer? I love you, Kenny, I love you."

I heard Daniella's voice breaking.

"Bye, Kenny."

Dad smiled softly. I moved the phone away, and Daniella and I cried. Dad loved Daniella's child-like nature, and I think he related to her hot-headed behaviours.

Over the next four days, the doctors increased his dose of morphine and other drugs to keep him comfortable.

He had biker mates visit him, and his sister, who could only handle one visit for fifteen minutes. I played him meditation music, or sound vibrations, to send him off with love. It felt like a soothing thing to do.

Just before my father died, I noticed his feet mottling, pale and red in patches, which reminded me of my fingers and toes before they 'died'. On the day of his death, the 3rd of July 2024, he was no longer responsive to hand-holding, yet I knew he could hear me.

"It's me, Dad. I love you and I forgive you for the past," I said.

At 8pm, the nurses called us, and Dad was gone.

Tarni, Alice, and I grabbed a bottle of champagne, a JBL speaker, and jumped in an Uber, heading back to room 11. As we entered the ward, the nurses looked at us with acknowledgement and sadness. There he was on his back, mouth open, his physical body still warm, and we all felt the impact of loss and grief. This is real, this is the relief we had been waiting for as tears rolled down our faces. There was something profound in that moment, seeing his relaxed face, his struggle over.

I walked towards his body. I wasn't afraid. I placed my hand gently on his forehead and stroked his long, soft, grey hair; he wanted to look like a biker right until the end. I touched his warm face with an enormous amount of love in my heart. I couldn't stop touching him. We all took turns saying goodbye. Alice played some country tunes, and we sat around his bed, drinking a glass of champagne. He would have loved that. The nurses walked in and out from time to time, quietly allowing us the time we needed. About an hour passed, and Alice said, "I want to wash his body; you both can help if you like."

Alice and Tarni are both nurses. My initial thought was, 'No way, I can't do that,' but what was I afraid of? Washing a dead man? Washing my father? It was personal, something I would not have thought of.

I jumped in to help. A special moment for us all. We pulled down the white cotton blanket to his waist and slowly took care to wash his cooling body. His face became paler. I took one last look at his tattoos, the one on his shoulder with the eagle crossing the sun, reminding me of my childhood days, when his strong shoulders would pick me up over his head and throw me into the ocean, and I would come back for more. We spent over an hour staring at him, washing him, loving him, touching him. I embraced his death with love and light.

29

Growth starts when comfort stops

When I reflect on an eagle crossing the sun, I see its wings expanded; the light is bright. A search for light, perhaps. Expanded, open and exposed. In this moment, there is stillness and warmth from the sun. The sun is quietly hidden, the eagle crosses and is then free from illumination until the next crossing.

Being a parentified child means you are the mother to your mother, your emotional needs are abandoned, and all your energy is consumed with making sure Mum is ok, a dumping ground for secrets and trauma. When would Mum break down? And when would Dad explode in anger? The eggshells that I walked on in my childhood were fractured into tiny pieces of loss, confusion and hypervigilance.

As a parentified child, I often chose partners who were unavailable. It was all I knew. I have since learnt to forgive myself, to lean into my flaws and embrace the thorns.

I'm sorry to my mother for leaving you in that hospital bed alone and lonely, I should have visited you more. I was also alone in your suffering, your depression and pain. I'm sorry for being resentful; I missed you and became a mother. There just wasn't room for me to be a child. I am sorry that the wheelchair I got for you didn't have a footrest. It was the only one left, and your thin legs pushed hard against the hospital floor as I also pushed hard to get you out the door. "Why can't I just have one cigarette?" You would say, nostrils flaring, your one last pleasure, one cheap Pall Mall cigarette. We sat in awkward, undigested anger. *Where was your brother? Why was it just me? It was just me because I felt responsible for you.*

It must've taken strength to starve yourself; it was self-loathing in its deepest form. It was a way of control and food restriction that kept you safe. However, your malnourished body was broken, your heart and mind afraid. You wanted to die a long time before 62, a lonely road for us both to walk, yet this was our contract. By the way, I loved our Friday nights with the evil KFC.

To Linda, my lover, my partner, I became your mother. The Lindas looked good. We were good for many years, but the ego and self-importance always ended in tears. We were young, drinking, smoking cigarettes, and partying. It was so much fun. The tantrums suffocated the light. What was safe? Did we really see each other? Let's get high, let's get drunk. We were blinded by our own trauma. We loved each other, and this has never been lost. Linda, thank you for the crazy workouts. Thank you for watching the sunrise with me. Thank you for loving Sunnie and Lola. Thank you for loving me. I'm grateful I got to love you, too.

To my wife, we figured it out. We had our share of pain and doubt; we got through it. You loved me through thick and thin. I saw you behind that façade you held so close. We became unbreakable, despite the odds that tried to break us; yet we grew stronger and survived. I'm sorry I couldn't set boundaries earlier. I couldn't see what was right in front of me; I had to learn my lessons. You are my person until I die. I will always try to speak my truth, to love myself and to love you. We just had to leave our partners; everything broke, everything shattered, and disgusting shame was all that mattered. I promise to never hit snooze again. I promise to listen to my heart, and I promise to listen to my guides. Could it be possible that the mosquito was my guide? I had to fulfil my curiosity and do some research. What I found startled me.

This tiny creature, so easy to swat away, has quietly

shaped the fate of humanity for millennia. In *The Mosquito: A Human History of Our Deadliest Predator*, Timothy C. Winegard describes how mosquitoes have carried parasites like malaria across empires and continents, leaving devastation in their wake. He referred to them as narcissists, and reading about them, it was chilling to think that this delicate insect - light enough to land unnoticed on skin - had been responsible for more human deaths than any war or weapon ever devised.

In his book, he says:

"We are at war with the mosquito. A swarming and consuming army of 110 trillion enemy mosquitoes patrols every inch of the globe save Antarctica, Iceland, the Seychelles, and a handful of French Polynesian micro-islands. The biting female warriors of this droning insect population are armed with at least fifteen lethal and debilitating biological weapons against our 7.7 billion humans, deploying suspect and often self-detrimental defensive capabilities. In fact, our defense budget for personal shields, sprays, and other deterrents to stymie her unrelenting raids has a rapidly rising annual revenue of $11 billion. And yet, her deadly offensive campaigns and crimes against humanity continue with reckless abandon. While our counterattacks are reducing the number of annual casualties she perpetrates, the mosquito remains the deadliest hunter of human beings on the planet. Last year, she slaughtered only 830,000 people. We sensible and wise Homo sapiens occupied

the runner-up #2 spot, slaying 580,000 of our own species..."

"...It has been one of the most universally recognizable and aggravating sounds on earth for 190 million years–the humming buzz of a mosquito. After a long day of hiking while camping with your family or friends, you quickly shower, settle into your lawn chair, crack an icecold beer, and exhale a deep, contented sigh. Before you can enjoy your first satisfying swig, however, you hear that all-too-familiar sound signaling the ambitious approach of your soon-to-be tormentors."

"...It is nearing dusk, her favorite time to feed. Although you heard her droning arrival, she gently lands on your ankle without detection, as she usually bites close to the ground. It's always a female, by the way. She conducts a tender, probing, ten-second reconnaissance, looking for a prime blood vessel. With her backside in the air, she steadies her crosshairs and zeros in with six sophisticated needles. She inserts two serrated mandible cutting blades (much like an electric carving knife with two blades shifting back and forth), and saws into your skin, while two other retractors open a passage for the proboscis, a hypodermic syringe that emerges from its protective sheath. With this straw she starts to suck 3-5 milligrams of your blood, immediately excreting its water, while condensing its 20% protein content. All the while, a sixth needle is pumping in saliva that contains an anticoagulant preventing your blood *from clotting at the puncture site..."*

"... the two most dangerous and widespread contenders battling for hegemony of your health and life -vivax and falciparum."

"The malaria parasite roosting in your liver will traverse through an impressive seven-stage life cycle. It must have multiple hosts to survive and procreate—the mosquito and an army of secondary vectors: humans, apes, rats, bats, rabbits, porcupines, squirrels, a volery of birds, a congress of amphibians and reptiles, and a swarm of others."

"Unfortunately, you are that host. Following that fateful mosquito bite, this miscreant will mutate and reproduce inside your liver for one to two weeks, during which time you will show no symptoms. A toxic army of this new form of the parasite will then explode out of your liver and invade your bloodstream."

"The parasites attach to your red blood cells, quickly penetrate the outer defenses, and feast on the inner hemoglobin. Inside the blood cell, they undergo another metamorphosis and reproductive cycle. Engorged blood cells eventually burst, spewing both a duplicate form, which marches forward to attack fresh new blood cells, and also a new "asexual" form

that relaxedly floats in your bloodstream, waiting for mosquito transportation. The parasite is a shape-shifter, and it is precisely this genetic flexibility that makes it so difficult to eradicate or suppress with drugs or vaccines."

"You are now gravely ill with an orderly, clockwork progression of chills followed by a mercury-driving fever touching 106 degrees. This full blown cyclical malarial episode has you in its firm grip and you are at the mercy of the parasite. Lying prostrate and agonizingly helpless on sweat-soaked sheets, you twitch and fumble, curse and moan. You look down and notice that your spleen and liver are visibly enlarged, your skin has the yellowing patina of jaundice, and you vomit sporadically. Your mind-melting fever will relapse at precise intervals with each new burst and invasion of the parasite from your blood cells. The fever then subsides while the parasite eats and reproduces inside new blood cells."

For me, the mosquito had shifted from being an irritant in the night to something else entirely - a teacher. Its persistence, its ability to adapt, its silent and devastating impact - all of it spoke to the hidden forces shaping not just my history, but also the unseen battles within myself.

A couple of weeks after Dad's death, I was walking along the beach in Byron Bay with Tarni and Nibbles. I looked to the clear blue sky to see an eagle crossing the path of the sun. Its wings highlighted the brown and cream hues as the huge bird slowly passed above me. It was a precise moment.

"Hi, Dad," I said to the sky. "Thanks for watching over me."

The hairs on my arms were raised in gratitude just as they did way back when I felt the awe of Gemma the elephant in Cambodia.

I also decided to look at the mosquito as a spiritual totem. I had never thought a mosquito could be the bearer of a message, or even worse, a spirit guide. I recalled a particular day when I was sitting at my desk, feeling stuck in my writing. I put my pen down and looked out at the enormous array of Australian native trees, and as I breathed in the expanse of nature, I heard a mosquito buzzing in my ear. I waved my hand back and forth, attempting to get rid of her.

"In Japan, mosquitoes are reincarnations of deceased people."

I stopped flapping her away, and within minutes, the mosquito landed on my wrist and stayed long enough for me to take a photo. To me, it was Mum; she was around. "Hi Mum," I said.

Enthusiastically, I started reading further.

"As your animal ally, a mosquito comes to 'bug' in someone's ear, alerting them that potential problems are afoot. Questions

arise, like are you disturbed by someone or something, but try to swat it away? When the mosquito buzzes into your life as a spirit animal, it bears one of several messages:

1. *Paying too much attention to superficial matters*
2. *Look hard at the company you keep. Are they sucking you dry?*
3. *Some people don't recognise when something is bothering them, because they have been stuck in a toxic environment for so long that it feels normal.*
4. *Figure out what needs to change, and make alterations, then take a bite out of life's joy again.*
5. *What you block can make you uneasy like a mosquito.*

In private times, you are a deep thinker with profound sentiments. Watch you don't get yourself so tangled up in a quandary that everything seems out of whack. You live vibrantly, love deeply and feel intensely. As you know yourself and honour yourself, you'll find the negative tendencies fade away."

I resonated with all of it.

Could the mosquito be my totem animal?

Most of us hate mozzies, and I certainly didn't have any interest in mosquitoes, nor in their intelligence or world history. The mosquito was just the annoying pest at the barbecue that everyone wanted to kill. In fact, the mosquito would often consume our attention, lighting coils, dousing ourselves with toxic repellents or being amazed at how many bites you got just walking out the back door, not to mention the constant itching; the constant reminder.

Perhaps Timothy C. Winegard was right: the mosquito is indeed a narcissist. So why the sudden interest in mosquitoes? Because the mosquito and I got into a battle. She cracked me open, I grew into a different person, and literally broke me. I still consider myself a stoic, so I pull a card from a pack of cards; Stoicism, a homage to one of the most relevant philosophies ever devised.

"When we call someone a 'stoic', it is about the way they handle the challenges in life with resilience and calm. The Stoics accepted that they could not control the world. In this sense, they despised traditional politics of warfare; they believed that true serenity could only be discovered through working on ones mind."

I am not my body; I am a servant to my mind. I am love, not seeking it externally, but recognising it as part of my inner nature. I observe without judgment; I speak without arrogance. I teach love. I become love. I am 'The Man In The Mirror'.

About the Author

Shelley is an Australian-born emerging writer. She is a former police officer and psychotherapist. She has a keen interest in a number of healing modalities and their impact on mental and physical health.

Shelley has been living with a disability since 2018 and recently spoke at the Asia Pacific Writers Translators in Thailand on "Writing Through Trauma".

Only Joy Bites is her debut book.

Follow Shelley on Instagram
@Shelley11_11

References

1. Brown, Brene (2010) *The Gifts of Imperfection* Hazeldon: USA

2. Geshe Kelsang Gyatso (1992). *Introduction to Buddhism: An Explanation of the Buddhist Way of Life*, Tharpa Publications: England and New York

3. Geshe Kelsang Gyatso (2005). *How to Solve Our Human Problems: The Four Noble Truths* Tharpa Publications: England and New York

4. Dayton, T. (2000). *Trauma and Addiction: Ending the Pain Through Emotional Literacy*

5. Dr Roger Cole (2013) *Mission of Love*, Hachette Australia

6. Quoted extracts from Timothy C. Winegard (2019): *A Human History of Our Deadliest Predator*, Penguin

7. Sepsis- https://www.mayoclinic.org/diseases-conditions/sepsis/symptoms-causes/syc-20351214 Accessed 3/5/2024

8. The Benefits of Human Touch https://allrelationshipmatters.com.au/insights-healthy-relationships/human-touch

9. Whatismyspiritanimal.com: Mosquito. https://whatismyspiritanimal.com/spirit-totem-power-animal-meanings/insects/?srsltid=AfmBOooiZ9j878m-YZX7sfjibn-JrIKVBAb67qhNu-uRtE2vFn_gFk_wA Accessed 3/5/2024

10. Elisabeth Kubler Ross (2014) *On Death and Dying* Scribner Book Company US

11. "Resilience" meaning referenced from Oxford English Dictionary (2010), OUP Oxford.

Acknowledgements

I would like to acknowledge all the amazing people who have walked this journey with me, all the crazy times and all the love that helped me survive and heal.

To all of my friends, you have shown up and allowed me to rebuild my life with strength and courage.

I also want to acknowledge the ongoing support of my physicians, personal trainers and healers who have made an incredible impact on how I live my life today.

www.ingramcontent.com/pod-product-compliance
Lightning Source LLC
Chambersburg PA
CBHW020523080526
44583CB00013B/715